WITHDRAWN

The Russo-Chinese
Borderlands

Zone of Peaceful Contact or Potential Conflict?

(Second Edition)

by W. A. DOUGLAS JACKSON

**Professor of Geography
University of Washington**

A SEARCHLIGHT ORIGINAL

under the general editorship of

G. ETZEL PEARCY
The Geographer
U. S. Department of State

GEORGE W. HOFFMAN
Professor of Geography
University of Texas

D. VAN NOSTRAND COMPANY, INC.

PRINCETON, NEW JERSEY

TORONTO   LONDON

MELBOURNE

VAN NOSTRAND REGIONAL OFFICES:
New York, Chicago, San Francisco

D. VAN NOSTRAND COMPANY, LTD., *London*

D. VAN NOSTRAND COMPANY (Canada), LTD., *Toronto*

D. VAN NOSTRAND AUSTRALIA PTY. LTD., *Melbourne*

Library of Congress Catalog Card No. 68–9548

PRINTED IN THE UNITED STATES OF AMERICA

Preface to the Second Edition

W HEN the first edition of *The Russo-Chinese Borderlands* went to the press early in 1962, Sino-Soviet ideological differences had not reached the level of an official, publicly acknowledged dispute. Even where those differences pertained to matters of fundamental significance, it was assumed by many Western writers that they would not disrupt the revolutionary alliance between Russia and the new China.

A Sino-Soviet relationship founded on the mutual commitment to Marxism-Leninism created a power situation in Eurasia, the implications of which were most disturbing for the West. With Moscow serving as the nerve center for the entire apparatus, the lands and peoples from East Germany to North Vietnam lay in the grip of Communism, a movement dedicated to the destruction of Western values and organization. Despite some evidences of unrest, especially in Eastern Europe, the USSR, through its satellite and allied regimes, seemed firmly in control of the Communist bloc. Moreover, the relative quiet in the Russo-Chinese borderlands tended to confirm the notion that the Sino-Soviet boundary was, indeed, a "friendship" boundary insuring the stability of the lands it touched. Communist theorists never tired of pointing to the fraternal relations between the USSR and the Chinese People's Republic (CPR) as proof of the thesis that between socialist countries conflict is impossible and that wars are the result of competition or the imperialism of the capitalist countries.

However, with the advantage of the hindsight afforded by the

1

past six years, it is now clearly evident to us that a variety of issues, not all of a purely ideological nature, did in fact disturb the calm of the Sino-Soviet relationship in the decade following the revolution in China. That upheaval did not wipe clean the record of history. The ideological marriage of Russia and the new China concealed, but did not eliminate, many problems with roots deep in the past. And every educated Chinese citizen easily remembered that the modern boundaries of China in the west and north had been formed under Russian pressure, be it Tsarist or Soviet.

The delineation of the Sino-Soviet boundary was not so much a cause for friction as was China's firm determination to gain control of the outer provinces, especially in the northwest where Russian influence had been strong and the native peoples restive if not outright hostile to the Chinese. After 1949 Russian influence was reduced and (for the most part) ultimately eliminated in Manchuria and Inner Mongolia, though it continued to be a factor in the internal affairs of Sinkiang, whose economic potential assumed a new dimension with the discovery of substantial deposits of oil not far from the Soviet boundary. Outer Mongolia, the Mongolian People's Republic, is little more than a region of the Soviet Union. Though Peking formally recognized the independence of the republic, it provided economic aid and assistance in what seemed an obvious intent to challenge Soviet hegemony and replace it with Chinese.

As the dispute between USSR and CPR deepened, the outside world became more fully aware of the polycentrist tendencies within the Communist bloc. Not only was Moscow's claim to central authority contested, but the polemic that ensued revealed how strong was the latent resentment of the Chinese toward the Russians. In 1963 this resentment culminated in claims by the Chinese Communists for the return of several hundred thousand square miles of territory ceded to Russia under the "unequal" treaties of the latter half of the 19th century.

The Chinese claims not only tended to link the Soviet regime with the Tsarist, but also may have encouraged the notion among the lesser developed nations of the world that Russia belonged in the camp of the European imperialists. Moreover, the raising of boundary questions in Asia opened a Pandora's box for Moscow in Eastern Europe. As a result of World War II, the Soviet frontier had been advanced westward, chiefly at the expense of Poland and a dismembered Germany. A strong bid for the surrender of Soviet territory in Asia could strengthen those forces seeking a revision of boundaries in Eastern Europe.

The question of borderlands and lost territories did not create the Sino-Soviet dispute; rather, the dissension focused attention on the existence of territorial problems of long standing. With the Chinese demands for the return of ceded territory, however, Sino-Soviet relationships took a turn for the worse, producing a polemic rarely found among nations at peace.

The tantalizing question arising out of these developments concern the motives of the Chinese Communists. The insistence by Peking on paramountcy in her own borderlands is understandable, but what prompted the claims to territories lost a century ago? True, the 19th-century treaties had been imposed by an aggressive Tsarist Russia on a weakening Manchu Dynasty; even so Imperial Chinese hegemony over much of the surrendered territory had been more nominal than real.

Peking may not believe that it can force the Soviet Union to surrender the lost territories, but by pressing the larger claim it may be satisfied with achieving some boundary rectification, possibly in the Pamirs and in the Far East, and with insuring the final removal of Soviet influence in the outer provinces. Once these objectives have been reached, stability in the borderlands may be realized. In the meantime, the Chinese Communists have found a weapon with which to embarrass their powerful neighbor to the north, and its use has tormented Moscow as only a frontier question can. In the past, whenever it suited her purpose, Russia had given little heed to the sanctity of international boundaries—whether they had been in China, Tannu-Tuva, Eastern Europe, or Iranian Azerbaydzhan.

Now Moscow must seek a legalistic defense of its own borders. Nations, as B. M. Klimenko has written, must avoid the use of force for the changing or rectification of "historically formed" frontiers.[1]

This text, like that of the first edition, is concerned primarily with the history and political geography of the lands along the Russo-Chinese international boundary. It has been completely rewritten in the light of recent developments. As before it is the hope of the author not only to introduce the reader to these little known and fascinating regions, but also to further illuminate the nature of the Sino-Soviet relationship.

W. A. DOUGLAS JACKSON

[1] B. M. Klimenko, *Frontiers: A Problem of Peace,* Moscow: International Affairs Press, cited in *Central Asian Review,* Vol. XIII, No. 1, 1965, pp. 2–3.

Contents

*Sinkiang, 120; Implications of the Sino-Soviet Boundary
Problems for Eastern Europe, 124; The Course of the Mongolian People's Republic, 129*

Maps (Following p. 78)

Tables

1   *The Borderlands and their Geographical Characteristics*

I N order to appreciate the geographical characteristics of the Russo-Chinese borderlands and to understand something of their complexity and of their contribution to the Sino-
Soviet dispute, it is convenient to divide them into three distinct
sectors. These sectors may be designated Inner Asia, the Far East,
and Mongolia.

In Inner Asia, the Sino-Soviet boundary is some 2,000 miles long
and extends from the lofty Pamirs to the Altay Mountains (Figure
1). The actual line of demarcation cuts rather arbitrarily over
mountains and across valleys, from alpine tundra to lowland wastes
and dry steppes. To the west of the line lie the republics of Soviet
Central Asia and Kazakhstan, a region generally known in the
latter half of the 19th century as Russian Turkestan. To the east
is Sinkiang, or "new province," now called the Sinkiang-Uighur
Autonomous Region after the Uighurs, a Turkic people and the
largest non-Sinic ethnic group in this, the northwestern region of
Communist China.

East of the Altay is the Mongolian sector. Here the Mongolian
People's Republic (MPR), historically known as Outer Mongolia,
is interposed, like a buffer, between the Soviet Union and Communist China. The landlocked republic consists essentially of a
tilted plateau, whose elevation decreases generally from northwest to
southeast. On the north, for about 1,500 miles, Mongolia is bounded
by Siberia, i.e., between the Altay in the west to beyond Lake Baykal
in the east. The Mongolian boundary with China commences also

7

in the Altay; after extending in a broad concave arc across the Gobi, it again reaches the Siberian boundary a short distance east of the Nerchinsk Range.

Although the MPR has gained international recognition and a seat in the United Nations, its situation prohibits freedom of action. From the early 1920's to the mid-1950's, Mongolia was little more than a Soviet satellite. Except for a short period when the influence of Peking seemed to be on the increase, Mongolia has insisted on its attachment to the Soviet position in the current Sino-Soviet dispute. In turn, Soviet leaders have affirmed, in effect, that any threat to the present status of Mongolia would constitute a threat to Soviet interests and, ultimately, to Soviet Siberia. Thus, for all practical purposes, the Sino-Mongolian boundary represents the outer perimeter of Soviet defense.

The Far Eastern sector, to the east of Mongolia, occupies for the most part the basin of the Amur River. Indeed, the Amur and its tributaries, the Argun and the Ussuri, constitute the physical boundary between Trans-Baykalia and the Soviet Far East on the one hand, and the Chinese Northeast Region, or Manchuria, on the other.

THE INNER ASIAN SECTOR

The division of the arid lands of Inner Asia between Russia and China was effected by a series of treaties and agreements drawn up between 1860 and 1884, following the occupancy and conquest of much of the Aral Sea basin by the forces of Tsarist Russia. Although the Russians took advantage of their position, not only before the Revolution but afterward as well, to encroach upon Sinkiang for political or economic advantage, the international boundary—at least on Russian or Western maps—has remained unchanged for almost a century. Chinese maps, on the other hand, have either shown much of the Pamir boundary as still to be defined or have shown it several hundred miles to the west of its present location, thus putting a large part of the high plateau within Sinkiang. The worsening of Sino-Soviet relations, too, not only has given rise to border violations and tension in Inner Asia, but has brought the expression of Chinese Communist claims to territory lost to Russia in the last century. Thus, the Chinese Communists would seem to regard much of the Inner Asian boundary as unsatisfactory and a matter for future renegotiation.

The Pamir region, as a study of the map will reveal, is indeed a strategic one (Figure 2). To the south lie Afghanistan and, beyond it, Kashmir, which is in dispute between India and Pakistan. The Russian boundary with Afghanistan, demarcated by a joint Anglo-Russian commission in 1895, left Wakhan in Afghan hands as a buffer between the Russian and British Empires. At one point, the airline distance across Wakhan between Russia and Kashmir is only eight miles. On the Indo-Pakistani side, however, the Wakhan Valley is buttressed by the mighty Hindu Kush (mountains), which rise to 25,000 feet.

The presence of British troops in the subcontinent—and of the British fleet beyond—guaranteed the stability of the Pamir boundaries. But this power was removed in 1948 when Pakistan and India emerged as independent states, and their joint strength since has been lessened as a result of their conflict over Kashmir. Although the Russians have at least encouraged secessionist feeling among the Pathans who live in Pakistan's northwest, no evidence exists of a direct threat to Pakistan from the USSR. On the other hand, China's international posture has from time to time provoked alarm throughout much of the subcontinent. The discovery in 1959 that the Chinese Communist regime had built a road across India's Outer Ladakh region to link Sinkiang and Tibet caused much consternation in India. Subsequently, of course, this event was followed by outright hostilities between the two powers in the remote rugged Indian border country. The Pakistanis, on the other hand, because of their long-standing conflict with India over Kashmir were able to negotiate in 1962–63 an agreement with Peking which led to a more precise demarcation of the boundary with Sinkiang. More-

over, early in 1965 it was reported that the caravan route from
Gilgit to Sinkiang through the high mountain country had been
reopened. Still, if the Chinese Communists should gain control
of the major passes through the Karakorum, a serious threat to
Pakistan's very existence as an independent state might ensue.

The Pamirs have been described as the roof of the world. To
the late Soviet geographer, L. S. Berg, they were "a miniature
Tibet," where the ranges reach 16,000 to 18,000 feet in elevation.
Snow lies on the higher peaks all year round, but it is for the most
part a dry barren land. Yet it was up over these lofty mountains
from Kashmir that the 13th-century Venetian traveler, Marco Polo,
came on his remarkable journey to the fabled court of Kublai Khan,
nephew of Genghis Khan.[1]

The present Sino-Soviet boundary through the eastern part of the
plateau, as shown on Soviet maps, is probably not far to the east
of Marco Polo's route. The Soviet Pamir lies within the Gorno-
Badakhshan Autonomous Oblast, a subordinate unit of the
Tadzhik Soviet Socialist Republic. The Tadzhiks are ethnically related to the Iranians as well as to some of the peoples to the south
in Afghanistan. Although the Tadzhik Republic has nearly two
million inhabitants, the bulk of the population lives in the valleys
of the Vakhsh and Amu-Darya Rivers to the west, leaving the high
plateau sparsely occupied.

Marco Polo probably followed an old trail across the plateau, but
today a motor road makes travel less tedious. Until recently there
was no transport route through or into the Chinese Pamir, but in
the last few years the Chinese Communists have built a road southwest from Kashgar to Puli, 200 miles distant. Known as the Pamir
Road, it heads in the direction of the Karakorum passes and Pakistan's Gilgit Agency. Puli is the capital of the Tash Kurghan
Tadzhik Autonomous Hsien, a subordinate ethnic administrative
area in Sinkiang whose inhabitants are Sarikola Tadzhiks and, as
Ismaeli Muslims, followers of the Aga Khan.

[1] *The Travels of Marco Polo,* New York: Boni and Liveright, 1926, p. 66.

As shown on Soviet maps, the international boundary extends northward from the Pamirs into the Trans-Alay Ranges, which bound the high plateau on the north. Beyond the Trans-Alay lies a broad upland valley, drained primarily to the west by the Kyzylsu. Much of this territory has been inhabited for centuries by Kirgiz pastoralists. Administration of the area, however, falls within the Soviet Kirgiz Republic, on the one hand, and the Chinese Kyzylsu Kirgiz Autonomous Chu, or district, on the other.

From the upland basin, the Sino-Soviet boundary turns eastward into the Tien-Shan where, for the most part, it follows the crest of the Kokshaal-Tau Range (Figure 2). Extending for nearly 2,000 miles east-west through Inner Asia, the Tien-Shan are a mass of ranges of varying ages, containing small enclosed basins. The highest peak is found in the central Khan-Tengri Range, Mt. Pobeda (24,400 feet), just inside the Kirgiz SSR. There are several passes through the high mountain complex, including the Kyzylsu and the Torugart (12,700 feet), both of which are crossed by motor roads. On his way to Kashgar, Marco Polo descended into the dry Tarim Basin probably by way of the Kyzylsu, which affords the most direct approach to the historic oasis from the Pamirs.

On the Soviet side of the boundary, the Tien-Shan fall primarily within the Kirgiz SSR. However, the largest and most fertile basin within the entire system, known as Fergana, lies considerably to the west, within the Uzbek Republic. Watered by the Syr-Darya and its principal tributary, the Naryn, the Fergana Valley has been a center of culture and crop cultivation for centuries. The Uzbeks, a Turkic people named after Uzbek, a descendant of Genghis Khan and onetime (1312–40) Khan of the Golden Horde, have occupied the lowlands between the Syr-Darya and the Amu-Darya since the 15th century. There, in the centuries that followed, they formed the Emirate of Bukhara and the Khanate of Khorczm, or Khiva. Somewhat later, in the Fergana Valley, the Khanate of Kokand took shape.

The Russian conquest of Turkestan in the 19th century was accompanied by a significant increase in the cultivation of cotton, through the introduction of American varieties and the expansion of irrigation facilities. By 1913 Turkestan supplied approximately half the cotton processed in the mills of the Moscow region compared to only 30 percent in 1890. Following the Bolshevik Revolution, and particularly in the 1930's, the cotton acreage in Soviet Central Asia underwênt a substantial increase, particularly with the construction of the Stalin Great Fergana Canal. The latter enhanced the agricultural importance of Fergana, making it in effect the "cotton bowl" of the USSR.

In Sinkiang, the Tien-Shan, known to the Chinese as the "Heavenly Mountains," constitute a major geographic feature and, according to Owen Lattimore, "The Key to Chinese Turkestan." [2] To the north of the Tien-Shan lies Dzhungaria; to the south is the Tarim Basin.

The larger Tarim Basin is one of the driest regions of Asia. Indeed, it could be said that the extensive Takla-Makan—which occupies the core of the basin—is nearly rainless, owing to the barrier against moisture-bearing winds presented by the high mountains that border it on the south (Kun Lun), on the west (the Pamirs), and on the north (Tien-Shan).[3] Yet life has ancient roots in the Tarim Basin, centered in the oases that are scattered around the huge wasteland at the base of the mountains. Glacier-fed streams descending from the mountains and, to some extent, connected by the Tarim River have afforded water, which has sustained cultivation. Kashgar is the most important oasis, but Yarkend and Khotan beneath the lofty Kun Lun, and Aksu beneath the Tien-Shan, are also significant. Today, Kashgar, with a population of several hundred thousand, is the westernmost city of modern China, a

[2] Owen Lattimore, *Inner Asian Frontiers of China,* New York: American Geographical Society, 1940; 2nd edition, 1951, p. 151.

[3] Despite the aridity, the Chinese geographer Jen Yu-ti reported in 1964 that some reclamation had taken place in the heart of the desert, where there were lakes fed by underground streams, which in turn had produced a grass vegetation. See his *A Concise Geography of China,* Peking: Foreign Language Press, 1964, pp. 207–208.

growing industrial center and the administrative capital of south-western Sinkiang, whose population amounts probably to over three million. Because of the aridity and sparse pastures in the lowlands, grazing is confined essentially to the uplands, where cattle-breeding Tadzhiks and Kirgiz pastoralists are found. The latter are the more numerous and in 1961, according to the *Soviet Atlas of Peoples of the World,* numbered 85,000. In the oases, the predominant ethnic group is Uighur. Although the ethnonym "Uighur" is an historic one (found in inscriptions on eighth and ninth century stone markers along the Orkhon River in Mongolia),[4] it was officially adopted for the native Turkic dwellers of the Tarim oases only in 1921. Until that date, these people called themselves Kashgarians, or Khotanians, after the locality in which they lived. The number of Chinese in the Tarim Basin is not known, but their numbers have undoubtedly increased in recent years. Much of the increase presumably represents administrative and military personnel.

Several motor roads through the high mountain passes to the west, as noted above, link the Tarim Basin with the Soviet Union. The oasis settlements at the base of the encircling mountains are also joined by roads. Extending eastward along the foot of the Altyn Tagh from the city of Kashgar is the Silk Road, which Marco Polo followed on his way to Peking. Passing salty Lob-Nor in the eastern part of the territory, the historic traveler entered China proper through the Kansu Corridor. In those days, the Road permitted a trade in exotic wares between the Orient and the Mediterranean. In the past decade, the Chinese Communists have built a railway through the corridor in an effort to develop the resources and economy of Sinkiang. Another historic road, known as "The Dry Run," marches along the southern piedmont of the Tien-Shan, but at the eastern end of the mountains it turns north into the Turfan Depression. There it joins the Dzhungarian Road, which links Urumchi and Hami to the Kansu Corridor. Urumchi is the major

---

[4] *Narody Sredney Azii i Kazakhstana,* Moscow, 1963, Vol. II, p. 489.

city of Sinkiang, while Hami is the easternmost. These roads have probably been improved, and additional parallel rail lines are to be constructed. Finally, south from Kashgar the Communists have built a motor road through Outer Ladakh into Tibet.

Approaching the Ili River, the Sino-Soviet boundary next crosses the "corridor area" of Inner Asia. Greater precipitation and moisture north of the Tien-Shan than south of them, and the presence of an almost continuous belt of good pastures along the northern slopes of the mountains, have made possible the large movements of nomads that contributed so much to the shaping of the history of the peoples, especially those of the lands to the west. It was along this route, in the 13th century, that the Mongol tribes under Genghis Khan came. Boundaries that cross corridors, particularly if they are river valleys, have traditionally been militarily vulnerable. The "highways" of western Dzhungaria demonstrate this fact most dramatically. Indeed, as General Kuropatkin, administrator of Russian Turkestan, noted in 1917, the most vulnerable part of the entire Russian frontier with China lay in the Inner Asian sector.

Immediately to the north of the main mass of the Tien-Shan lies the Ili Valley, bounded by the Narat and Borokhoro Ranges. Confined by the ranges at its eastern end, the basin widens toward the west, making it more accessible to Russia than to China. The Ili, rising inside Sinkiang, drains into Lake Balkhash in Soviet Kazakhstan, nearly a thousand miles to the west. Not far inside the USSR, to the south of the Ili on the Turkestan-Siberian Railway, is Alma-Ata, the capital of the Kazakh SSR. Founded over a century ago, it contains more than 625,000 inhabitants, predominantly Russian in origin. From its position, the city is able to command the western approach to the upper Ili. Between Alma-Ata and the Sino-Soviet boundary are a number of Uighur settlements, established in the latter years of the 19th century, following Russian withdrawal from the upper Ili.

The largest city on the Chinese Ili is Kuldja or Ining, a fortress town, with a population well over 110,000. The territory around Kuldja forms the Chapchal Sibo Autonomous Hsien, although the

Sibos, a Tungus-Manchurian people, number only 23,000. Because of their close association with the Uighurs and other Turkic peoples, the Sibos have been strongly Turkicized. In the past, the Ili was used by the Chinese emperor as a region of exile for political dissenters.

From Kuldja a good motor road leads westward to the boundary, toward Soviet Kazakhstan and the Turk-Sib Railway. The distance from Kuldja to the Soviet railhead is only 200 miles, but until recent years a three-month caravan trip was necessary to reach the nearest Chinese station 1,200 miles to the east. Another motor road leads northward over the Borokhoro Range into the Dzhungarian Basin, where it meets the main Dzhungarian Road. The Ili River also has served as an artery of trade, the navigational season extending from the end of March to the beginning of November. Although the motor road across the boundary now offers the advantage of direct transport, the Ili has, until recently, carried up to 35,000 tons of freight annually. This tonnage included agricultural machinery, cement, iron ore, and also oil.

North of the Ili Basin, the Sino-Soviet boundary climbs into the Dzhungarian Ala-Tau, an east-west trending range that reaches elevations of over 15,000 feet. Following the crest of the range, the boundary drops abruptly into a deep, low-lying depression 46 miles long, bounded on the north by the Barlik Maili Range. This is the historic Dzhungarian Gate. By way of Lakes Ebi-Nur and Alakol, it is in direct line with the major oases of Dzhungaria and, to the west of the international boundary, Lake Balkhash. Before the worsening of Sino-Soviet relations, there was a joint plan to link Kazakhstan and Sinkiang by rail at the Dzhungarian Gate. The Soviet regime lost no time in constructing a line from Aktogay on the Turk-Sib Railway the short distance to the boundary. But the Chinese authorities, since extending the Lanchow-Sinkiang rail line to the west of Urumchi, have not seen fit to go any farther.[5]

[5] For a discussion of the projected railway, see Chang Kuei-sheng, "The Changing Railroad Pattern in Mainland China," *Geographical Review*, Vol. LI, No. 4, 1961, esp. p. 542.

Not far to the northeast, but beyond the Barlik Maili, the boundary again crosses open steppe. Here, a good motor road, passing Chuguchak (or T'a-ch'eng), affords connection between northwestern Dzhungaria and Ayaguz on the Turk-Sib Railway northeast of Aktogay. North of Chuguchak lies the Tarbagatay Range. The boundary extends into the mountains, turning east to follow, at 9,800 feet, the crest of the eastern half of the range. From there it runs north across the valley of the Black Irtysh before reaching the piedmont of the Altay. Between Alma-Ata and the Tarbagatay Range, on the Soviet side, are the Russian settlements of the Semirechiye. But the territory to the north of the Tarbagatay, along the Black Irtysh, has been—until recently at least—essentially Kazakh land. However, the impressive electric power, mining, manufacturing and agricultural developments of Eastern Kazakh and Semipalatinsk Oblasts have resulted in further Russian inroads on Kazakh pasture lands.

The Black Irtysh River, rising in the Mongolian Altay to the east, drains into Lake Zaysan from whence the waters flow—via the Irtysh and subsequently the Ob—to the Arctic Ocean. In the past the Black Irtysh was an important route for the transport of minerals and other freight from northwestern Sinkiang to the USSR. A motor road runs along the valley, but as an artery of Russo-Chinese commerce it has been of considerably less importance than the more southerly routes, because the terrain through which it passes is dry and sparsely occupied.

Dzhungaria is a triangular-shaped basin occupying about 270,000 square miles. It is bounded on the northeast by the Mongolian Altay, on the south by the Tien-Shan, and on the northwest, as noted above, by ranges interspersed with depressed basins. With precipitation ranging from eight to ten inches annually in the lowlands and more in the uplands, Dzhungaria has been able to support a larger pastoral, but a smaller sedentary, population than Tarim. Many of the estimated 600,000 Kazakhs of Sinkiang (see Table I and Figure 4) live in the western half of Dzhungaria, principally in the

Ili Kazakh Autonomous Chu, where they have been compelled to engage in crop cultivation. In the past Kazakh tribes, whether of Soviet Central Asia or of Sinkiang, moved freely across the international boundary, especially in times of crisis. In recent years, what movement there has been has led in the direction of the Soviet Union. In 1962, for example, from 50,000 to 70,000 Kazakhs were said to have crossed into Kazakhstan, fleeing Chinese Communist attempts at collectivization or communization. Still others have been moved back from the boundary by the Peking regime to make way for Chinese colonization and settlement. The Sinkiang Kazakhs share a common language with Soviet Kazakhs and, until modern times, a common history. Though nominally Muslims, the Kazakhs have traditionally been lax in observing the practices of Islam.

Dzhungaria also contains up to 170,000 Mongols, found near the Tarbagatay Mountains and in the Tien-Shan, as well as near the Mongolian boundary. Like the Kazakhs, the Mongol peoples have also been settled and compelled to take up farm work. Like their counterparts in the MPR, the Sinkiang Mongols were followers of Lama Buddhism.

In addition to Kazakhs and Mongols, Dzhungaria also possesses a sizeable minority of Uighurs found principally in the oases about Manass, Urumchi, and Hami. The Manass River valley also contains a large portion of Sinkiang's Dungans or Chinese Muslims, known as Huei. Though the Dungans in Sinkiang numbered some 200,000 in 1953, in the following decade they may have increased by about 45,000.

According to Russian and Soviet ethnologists, the Dungans are basically Han Chinese who adopted Islam as a result of long contact with Arabs, Persians and Turkic peoples. Chinese scientists, on the other hand, identify the Dungans as migrants from the west, of mixed origin, who subsequently adopted the language and customs (and acquired some of the racial characteristics) of the surrounding Chinese. *The Soviet Atlas of Peoples of the World* estimates the number of Chinese Muslims at 3.5 million; apart from

the Sinkiang Dungans, the rest are found primarily in the Nin-
Hsia-Huei Autonomous Region and the nearby provinces of Kansu,
Shensi and Shansi.

The Soviet Dungan population is insignificant. According to the
Census of 1959, 21,900 lived in Central Asia, mainly in the Kazakh
and Kirgiz Republics. The Soviet minority is descended chiefly from
the Dungans who emigrated from Sinkiang after the Russian military withdrawal from the Ili in 1881.

TABLE I.

Ethnic Population of Sinkiang

Ethnic Group	1953	1961 Estimate
I Turkic		
1. Uighur	3,640,000	4,400,000 *
2. Kazakh	475,000	600,000 *
3. Kirgiz	70,000	85,000 *
4. Uzbek	8,000	17,000 *
5. Tatar	5,000	8,000 *
II Han Chinese	300,000	> 1,300,000
III Dungan (Huei)	200,000	c. 240,000
IV Mongol, Daur, others	120,000	< 170,000
V Manchu, Sibo	20,000	> 23,000
VI Russian	13,000	unknown
VII Tadzhik	15,000	c. 18,000
VIII Others	8,000	unknown
Total	4,874,000	c. 7,000,000

Sources: *East Turkic Review*, No. 4, 1960, p. 81; * *Atlas narodov mira*,
Moscow, 1964, pp. 141 ff.; Michael Freeberne, "Demographic and Economic
Changes in the Sinkiang Uighur Autonomous Region," *Population Studies*,
Vol. XX, No. 1, July 1966, pp. 103–124, esp. p. 111.

Apart from the Han Chinese, Sinkiang contains 12 different
ethnic groups. It is reported that since 1949 these groups together
have increased in population by 22.5 percent so that in 1965 they
represented 80 percent of the total population. Such data as these
are difficult to handle in view of the fact that there are no accurate

totals for 1949 and the size of the influx of Chinese into the area is not fully known. In 1953, there were only some 300,000 Chinese (Han) in Sinkiang (Table 1). By 1961 the number may have reached 1.3 million, and by the end of 1962 have risen to over 2.6 million following the migration of up to a million youths who were "channelled" into the northwest to open up wastelands. From 1963–65, too, some 50,000 Shanghai youths were sent out to Sinkiang. By 1965, therefore, the Chinese in Sinkiang probably accounted for more than a fifth of the total population. During the next two years the number of Chinese may have risen to over 3 million. If so, the total population of the entire region has grown from 4.9 million in 1953 to possibly 7 million in 1961, and to almost 9 million in 1967.

The extension of the railway to Urumchi and beyond, together with the improvement of surface transport generally, has contributed to economic advances: an expansion in mining, the erection of industrial establishments, an increase in electric power capacity and output, and a growth in the cultivated area. Sinkiang has a wide array of mineral resources, the full value and extent of which may not be realized for decades. Major oil fields are found at Karamai and Tushantzu.[6] There are widely scattered deposits of coal. Near Urumchi is an important oil shale reserve, still to be tapped. In addition to a number of low-grade iron deposits, Sinkiang possesses also significant deposits of barite, copper, lead, molybdenum, tungsten, zinc and uranium.

The expansion in the mining and power industries has been a major factor in the growth of manufacturing and in the increase in the number of urban-type settlements. In 1949 there were only 12 towns in Sinkiang with a population over 2,000; by 1964 there were 70. The increase in the population of Urumchi has been nothing less than spectacular. From 80,000 in 1949 Urumchi more than

---

[6] Chang, Kuei-sheng, "Geographical Basis for Industrial Development in Northwestern China," *Economic Geography*, Vol. 39, No. 4, Oct. 1963, pp. 343 ff.

doubled its inhabitants in the following decade, reaching about 500,000 in 1967.[7] Almost two-thirds of these are Han Chinese, with Uighurs accounting for only 20 percent and Dungans 15 percent of the total.

The influx of Chinese has led to a substantial expansion in the cultivated area. By 1967, approximately 8 million acres of land were under cultivation, compared to only 2.5–3 million in 1949.[8] Much of the increase has occurred in Dzhungaria, particularly in the Manass Valley. On the other hand, urban expansion in the oases has been at the expense of good irrigated land. Though the Chinese press has periodically reported good harvests of grain, it is doubtful that the region could ever be self-sufficient in foodstuffs—at least under present technology and assuming a continued in-migration of Chinese. Moreover, successful crop cultivation in Sinkiang depends heavily on irrigation, the potential for which in surface hydrology is not large. Major crops grown at present in the region include spring and winter wheat, corn, kaoliang, rice, millet, long-staple cotton (in the Tarim oases), and sugar beets (in Dzhungaria). Sinkiang is also noted for its fresh fruit and melons, i.e., Ili Valley apples, Hami melons, and Turfan seedless grapes.

Despite the material changes that have begun to transform the landscape of Sinkiang, the region's economy remains far less advanced than that of Soviet Central Asia. Before 1949, life had followed, for the most part, a pattern established in centuries past. Whatever economic direction there was had been supplied by Russia, Tsarist and Soviet, through the assumption at times of effective control over much of Dzhungaria. Moreover, the moderni-

[7] Michael Freeberne, "Demographic and Economic Changes in the Sinkiang-Uighur Autonomous Region," *Population Studies,* Vol. XX, No. 1, July 1966, p. 112; Herold J. Wiens, "The Historical and Geographical Role of Urumchi, Capital of Chinese Central Asia," *Annals,* A.A.G., Vol. 53, No. 4, Dec. 1963, pp. 441–464.

[8] Herold J. Wiens, "Cultivation Development and Expansion in China's Colonial Realm in Central Asia," *The Journal of Asian Studies,* Vol. XXVI, No. 1, Nov. 1966, pp. 67–88, esp. p. 82.

zation of the economy under the Chinese Communists has been built on the shaky foundations of native unrest.

The republics of Soviet Central Asia and Kazakhstan, by contrast, have experienced over 40 years of Soviet rule and at least a century of Russian domination. The entire region has been effectively integrated into the Soviet Union. Moreover, Russians and Ukrainians have migrated in large numbers into the area. Although a high natural rate of increase between 1959 and 1964 contributed to much of the six million increase in the population of the Soviet republics, in-migration, mainly of Slavs, accounted for about 1.4 million.

TABLE II.

Population of Soviet Central Asia and Kazakhstan

Republics	1959 Census	1965 Estimate (Jan. 1)
Uzbek	8,105,704	10,130,000
Kazakh	8,309,847	11,853,000
Kirgiz	2,065,837	2,569,000
Tadzhik	1,979,897	2,482,000
Turkmen	1,516,375	1,862,000
Total	22,977,660	28,896,000

Sources: *Itogi vsesoyuznoy perepisi naseleniya 1959 goda. SSSR.* Moscow, 1962, pp. 206–8; *Narodnoye khozyaystvo SSSR v 1964 g. Statisticheskiy yezhegodnik.* Moscow, 1965, pp. 16–17.

According to the Soviet census of 1959, of the ethnic groups in Soviet Central Asia and Kazakhstan, Eastern Slavs (Russians, Ukrainians and Byelorussians) accounted for 30 percent of the total (Tables 2 and 3), the Turkic peoples for over 55 percent, the Iranian Tadzhiks for less than one percent, and the other minorities for the rest. Although there have not been any substantial changes in the above ratios since 1959, Russians continue to outnumber Kazakhs in Kazakhstan and represent, with the other Slavs, significant minorities in the other republics. In the major cities—

centers of administration or industrial development—Russians form
large minorities if not outright majorities. Indeed, ever since its
founding, Alma-Ata, the capital of the Kazakh SSR, has been and
remains essentially a Russian city.

TABLE III.

Ethnic Groups in Soviet Central Asia and Kazakhstan
According to the Soviet Census of 1959

I	*Turkic*	
	1. Kazakh	3,232,403
	2. Uzbek	5,973,147
	3. Kirgiz	955,191
	4. Turkmen	985,643
	5. Karakalpak	168,274
	6. Tatar	799,840
	7. Azerbaydzhani	102,169
	8. Uighur	92,974
II	*Eastern Slavic*	
	1. Russian	6,213,830
	2. Ukrainian	1,034,965
	3. Byelorussian	121,596
III	*Iranians*	
	1. Tadzhik	1,377,760
IV	*Others*	
	1. Dungan	21,068
	2. Korean	212,472
	3. Jewish	137,495
	4. Polish	53,102
	5. Armenian	47,696

Sources: See Table II.

Whenever it has appeared, separatist feeling among the native
peoples has been suppressed, and Islam, the traditional religion of
the majority, has been severely proscribed. Few mosques are open.
Since 1928–29, the countryside has been collectivized and nomadism
eliminated, replaced by a form of controlled ranching with supple-
mental feeding, known as "otgonnoye" livestock raising. Before

the revolution, the Kazakh herdsmen resisted the inroads of the Russian peasant cultivator. Since then—and particularly since 1954 —their grassland patrimony has been further reduced by the ploughing of millions of acres of "waste" land throughout northern Kazakhstan. If the Kazakhs resisted this latest usurpation of their pastures, there is no evidence of it.

THE FAR EASTERN SECTOR

The Sino-Soviet boundary in the Far East has a uniformity that is not to be found in Inner Asia. For almost its entire length (approximately 2,000 miles), from the uplands of Trans-Baykalia to the Pacific Coast southwest of Vladivostok, it is a physical boundary consisting of the Amur River and its tributaries, the Argun and Ussuri.

The Far Eastern sector of the Sino-Soviet borderlands may be said to begin near the middle course of the Argun River, a short distance east of Manchouli, where the Chinese Eastern Railway crosses from Siberia into China or into the contemporary Inner Mongolian Autonomous Region. The construction and subsequent history of the railway demonstrates the exposed position of the Russian Trans-Ussuri territory. Above all, this position suggests that the natural hinterland of Vladivostok, the "fortress of the east," is not the Amur Valley to the north, but the lands to the northwest, i.e., the provinces of Manchuria and Inner Mongolia.

There are in the Far Eastern sector, an examination of Soviet and Chinese maps reveals, cartographic discrepancies in the tracing of the international boundary. Such discrepancies occur in the extreme west; near the junction of the Zeya and Amur Rivers; and at the confluence of the Amur and Ussuri Rivers. Indeed, since the entire length of the Far Eastern boundary has never been precisely delimited by mutual agreement, its status remains unsettled. Furthermore, as the Sino-Soviet controversy has deepened, Peking has indicated that there is an even greater issue at stake, namely the territory extending to the Pacific and northward as far as the

Stanovoy Mountains, surrendered by the Ch'ing Dynasty in the Treaties of Aigun and Peking.

On Soviet maps, the boundary between the Mongolian People's Republic and the middle reaches of the Argun represents a delineation achieved under the Tsitsihar Treaty of 1911. Originally the boundary here had been based on the 1727 Treaty of Kiakhta. By the 1911 treaty, however, the boundary was extended almost five miles into China along a sixty-mile front and, for the most part, drawn along the southerly channel of the Argun. The Tsitsihar agreement, however, was never recognized by the new republican government of China nor, subsequently, by the Chinese Communists. On Chinese maps, therefore, the international boundary lies somewhat farther to the north-northwest.

The distance from Mongolia to the Amur is about 600 miles. On the west, in the Soviet Union, lies Chita Oblast; on the east, the Inner Mongolian Autonomous Region. The union of the Argun and the Shilka, which enters from the uplands of central Chita, creates the Amur River proper, which forms the boundary for the next thousand miles. Between Mongolia and the Amur, sparsely-settled uplands dominate the borderlands. On the east, however, the plateau terminates in the Great Khingan Mountains. As the Amur flows past the hump of the Great Khingan, the elevation decreases and the landscape begins to reflect the influence of the Pacific. The high parched steppes, characteristic of much of the Inner Asian and, as we shall see, of the Mongolian sectors, give way imperceptibly to a greener, more luxuriant vegetation, reflecting the heavier summer precipitation, which prevails throughout the border lowlands of the Far East.

As the Amur continues its southeasterly course, the right or Chinese bank remains higher than the left. Low, rounded peaks (at 3,000 feet), which constitute the Little Khingan, extend eastward almost as far as the Sungari River, separating the Amur Valley from the Manchurian plain to the south. On the Soviet side, near the mouth of the Zeya River, which drains the rugged mountain ranges of eastern Amur Oblast, the uplands recede to the north, leaving a wide plain. The Zeya plain, or Zeya-Bureya plain, fertile, dotted with collective farms and comparatively well settled, serves as an important local granary. In a region where lowlands are at a minimum, the economic importance of the Zeya-Bureya plain should not be underestimated.

In 1858 a small parcel of land near the confluence of the Zeya and Amur, containing "64 settlements," was left under Manchu jurisdiction. In 1900 Russia seized the territory, driving the inhabitants out. Chinese Nationalist maps have continued to show, therefore, the left-bank territory as Chinese, although Chinese Communist maps do not.

Blagoveshchensk, the administrative center of Amur Oblast, is the major Russian city in the middle Amur Valley. By 1965 its population had reached 115,000. Situated on the Amur, it is linked by a branch line to the Trans-Siberian Railway, which runs along higher ground at some distance back from the river.

Toward the southeast the plain narrows and, below its confluence with the Bureya, the Amur is confined by highlands on both sides. Here the Little Khingan Mountains, which parallel the Amur on the Chinese side, are met by the Bureya Range (6,500 feet), which extends toward the Amur from the northeast. For a short distance the course of the river runs through a narrow gorge with sheer cliffs, a veritable Amur "Iron Gate." Beyond the Bureya and the Little Khingan, the Amur, swollen by the successive additions of the waters of the Sungari and the Ussuri, flows across an extensive level plain. Bogs and reed thickets are common along the river banks, and even land back from the river is poorly drained. Cultivation occurs mainly in areas of higher elevation and better natural drainage or where drainage has been improved.

East of the Bureya Range the Soviet border territory falls within Khabarovsk Kray or, more specifically, between the Bureya and the mouth of the Ussuri, the Jewish Autonomous Oblast, a subordinate unit within the kray. The Soviet attempt in the 1930's to create a

Jewish homeland in the Far East, known as Birobidzhan, to counteract the appeal of Zionism, was never an attractive alternative. While the oblast's present population is about 175,000, the Jewish element continues to remain relatively small.

On the Chinese side, from the Little Khingan to the Ussuri, the land is also poorly drained, especially along the lower Sungari, and Chinese settlement is sparse. In recent years, however, Chinese migrants have begun to take up land near the Amur and to make improvements. To the south, in the Manchurian plain, the population density swells dramatically. Some forty million acres of Manchuria's fertile black soil have already been brought under cultivation, and it is possible that more may be ploughed. Throughout the plain densities reach 400 persons per square mile. The city of Harbin, where the Chinese Eastern Railway crosses the Sungari, has a population over 1.6 million. Several hundred miles to the south lies Mukden, with nearly 3 million, and the port of Dairen, with over 1.5 million. The Southern Manchurian industrial region is the largest in China. Finally, beyond the Great Wall to the southwest stretches the densely settled North China Plain.

At the confluence of the Amur and Ussuri Rivers, the Sino-Soviet boundary abruptly changes direction. Thereafter the Amur flows northeastward into the Pacific—past Khabarovsk, the chief Soviet city of the Far East with a population of 410,000, and Komsomolsk, the steel city, with 205,000 inhabitants. About twenty-five miles above Khabarovsk and the principal mouth of the Ussuri, the Amur is joined by the Kazakevicheva, a branch of the Ussuri. Between the Kazakevicheva and the main course of the Ussuri lie low, flat, uninhabited islands, which Chinese Communist maps include within the CPR. On Soviet maps, the boundary follows the Kazakevicheva to the Ussuri proper and thence south along the Ussuri and across marshy lowlands. From the Ussuri, the boundary reaches Lake Khanka via the Sungacha. It then crosses the northern part of the shallow lake and turns to the southwest through a series of low ranges, where, inland from the coast, it terminates. From that point to the Pacific, the USSR shares a common frontier with the Korean People's Republic.

East of the Ussuri, in the Maritime Kray, the terrain rises into the low, heavily wooded Sikhote-Alin. The range parallels the coast from north of the port city of Vladivostok to the mouth of the Amur, effectively cutting off the valley from the Pacific. The most concentrated Soviet settlement in Maritime Kray occurs in the Lake Khanka Plain and in and about Vladivostok, which has a population of 370,000. Along the coast there are scattered fishing villages and, it is reported, numerous naval and military installations. To the west of the Ussuri, in Manchuria, the Nadan Khada-Alin projects northward to separate the Ussuri and Lake Khanka Plains from the lower Sungari. The range is a continuation of the Eastern Manchurian Highlands that extend through the Sino-Soviet-Korean boundary zone.

In the middle of the 19th century, when the Russians took possession of the Amur, the lands on either side were inhabited by primitive tribes. These included Palaeo-Asiatics, such as the Nivkhi (Gilyaks), as well as Manchus and other groups belonging to the Tungus-Manchurian family. They lived by hunting, trapping, and fishing. To the west, in and beyond the Great Khingan, were various groups of Mongol pastoralists. The Russian advance into the Far East quickened the pace of Chinese settlement in Manchuria, while the Trans-Siberian Railway facilitated Russian occupancy from the west. Thus, today, with the exception of the Mongols in the Khingan region, the minority groups are of little significance. Even the Mongols total little more than 350,000, while the Manchus, numbering perhaps close to three million, have adopted the Chinese language.

The economic development of the Eastern Siberian and Far Eastern borderlands, however, pales alongside that of Manchuria. The Manchurian plain contains at least 7 percent of China's 700 million inhabitants (Table IV). The railways, part of which were built originally by the Tsarist government, have facilitated population movement and industrial development. While the mineral resources of the territory are not especially rich, they have been extensively developed in the south—mainly by the Japanese in the 1930's. Accordingly, Southern Manchuria, often called the "Ruhr of the Far East," has been given a broadly diversified manufacturing base, producing 30 percent of China's coal, at least 70 percent of its iron, and half of its electric power.

TABLE IV.

Population of Chinese Borderlands
(1957 estimate)

Manchuria	
Heilungkiang	14,860,000
Kirin	12,550,000
Liaoning	24,090,000
Inner Mongolia AR	9,200,000
Sinkiang-Uighur AR	5,640,000
Total	66,340,000

Source: *Encyclopaedia Britannica World Atlas,* Chicago, 1965, p. 222.

In contrast, the Soviet population of the Far Eastern borderlands probably totals little more than four million. Of these, however, more than half are urbanized, with the urban segment steadily growing. The countryside is sparsely occupied and has a rough appearance. Cropland amounts to little more than five million acres. Between 1954 and 1956, about a million acres of virgin and unused lands were ploughed, but one cannot assume that these lands are altogether suitable for crops. A short growing season, poorly-drained soils, and permafrost have been effective to date in restricting the agricultural potential. Thus, the Soviet Far Eastern population tends to cling to the Trans-Siberian Railway, on which it heavily depends; a short distance to the north stretch for many hundreds of miles almost impassable mountains. Furthermore, a rather weak industrial resource base inhibits the efforts of the Soviet regime to quicken development. Low quality iron ores have prevented the construction of a fully-integrated iron and steel mill at Komsomolsk. Although coal is found in quantity, its quality is of a medium grade for coking purposes. Sakhalin produces approximately 10 percent of Soviet oil, but its fields are the only significant producers in Siberia east of the Yenisey, and output is insufficient to meet the needs of both industry and the military. On the other hand, the water resources of the Amur Basin, as well as the overall forest wealth, are considerable, although relatively little exploitation of either has occurred to date.

THE MONGOLIAN SECTOR

Whereas in the Inner Asian and Far Eastern sectors of the borderland Sino-Soviet contact occurs along a common boundary, in the intervening Mongolian sector, the Mongolian People's Republic separates the two states (Figure 1). However, until very recently the southern boundary of the MPR, that is, the Sino-Mongolian boundary, might have been regarded as the *de facto* boundary between the USSR and the CPR because, from 1921 until 1955, the MPR was little more than a dependency or a satellite of the USSR, and all Chinese influence was excluded. In fact, according to the noted Mongolist Professor N. N. Poppe, who left the Soviet Union during World War II, there had been discussion in the Soviet Union before 1941 of plans to annex the MPR.

The Communist success in China, however, afforded the Mongols an opportunity to lessen their dependence on the USSR. Complete independence probably may never be achieved by land-locked Outer Mongolia, but the republic would gain if peace and stability were achieved in its relations with both the USSR and the CPR. For this reason—and obviously with the acquiescence of the Soviets— the Mongols initially were eager to accept economic aid and assistance from Peking. With support from both neighbors, the traditional face of historic Mongolia began to change. Ulan Bator, the capital, with a population in 1959 of 250,000, soon took on the appearance of a modern "bloc" city. With little opposition the felt yurt quickly yielded to the apartment house. Elsewhere in Mongolia bridges and roads were constructed and irrigation works installed. Much, if not all, the physical labor was performed by Chinese labor sent in from the CPR. After a five-year contract period, the Chinese were reportedly free to accept Mongol citizenship and settle in the republic, or to return home to China. In the mid-50's, from 12,000 to 16,000 Chinese laborers were thus employed in the republic. However, by 1964, as the Sino-Soviet dispute reached a level of antagonism rarely found among nations at peace, the number of Chinese laborers was reduced to above 6,000. The rest were completely withdrawn by the end of the year, when Mongol-Chinese talks about a new trade agreement were broken off.

Although the Mongols support the Soviet position in the ideological dispute with the Chinese Communists, the MPR has achieved international recognition through its position in the United Nations, which in turn has permitted a much wider circle of international contacts. For these reasons, the relationship of the MPR to the USSR, while obviously not one of equality, may be one of less dependence than that of a decade ago. Even so, the Soviet Union has indicated that any threat to Mongolia's boundaries and to its present status would represent a threat to the USSR.

The Mongolian People's Republic, with a population of approximately one million (Table V), consists essentially of a dry plateau, stretching for 1,470 miles from west to east and for about 780 miles from north to south at its widest extent. From an elevation of about 4,000 feet in the southeast, bordering Inner Mongolia, the republic tilts upward toward the northwest. Much of the southern half of the country lies within the Gobi Desert, a relatively flat wasteland. Ulan Bator lies near 5,000 feet. Toward the north and west, mountains such as the Khangai and the Mongolian Altay rise above the level of the plateau, the latter reaching heights of up to 15,000 feet.

Extensive grasslands cover much of the republic and contribute substantially to its economy. The pastures support millions of head of livestock, including cattle, sheep, goats, yaks, reindeer, horses, and camels. Through the years of the republic's history, the livestock and livestock products have been exported to the USSR. Because of aridity (precipitation averages about 10 inches annually),

TABLE V.

*Ethnic Groups in the Mongolian People's Republic
Based on 1961 Estimates*

Mongol	
Khalkha	755,000
Buryat	30,000
Darkhat	10,000
Oirat	65,000
Turkic	
Tuvinian and others	22,000
Kazakh	42,000
Tungus-Manchurian	
Evenki	1,000
Russian	15,000
Chinese	18,000
Total	958,000

Source: *Atlas narodov mira* (Moscow, 1964), pp. 141 ff. According to the census of 1956, Khalkhas comprised 75.6 percent of the total population; Buryats, 2.9 percent; Kazakhs, 4.3 percent; Chinese, 1.9 percent; and Russians, 1.6 percent. See I. Kh. Ovdiyenko, *Sovremennaya mongoliya,* Moscow, 1964, p. 42.

crop cultivation is restricted primarily to the north along the Selenga River. In the past decade, however, virgin lands in the east-central part of the republic (west of Ulan Bator) have been ploughed for wheat and corn with varying degrees of success. Near Karakorum, site of Genghis Khan's 13th-century capital, the waters of the Orkhon, a tributary of the Selenga, have been used to irrigate the land. Elsewhere, too, on a limited scale new irrigation projects have been implemented.

According to Owen Lattimore, the 2,700-mile long Sino-Mongolian boundary that separates Outer Mongolia from Inner Mongolia, an integral part of China, reflects a basic cleavage between the two areas which goes back to fundamental factors of geography and tribal history. The Mongols of Inner Mongolia, nearer to and thus more closely associated for many centuries with the intensive cultivators of the North China Plain, developed a markedly different character from that of the traditional nomads of the outer territory. Moreover, slightly more moist conditions than prevail in and north of the Gobi have made dry farming more successful. Although there are more Mongols in Inner Mongolia than in Outer Mongolia, Chinese migration and settlement in the former region have proceeded to such an extent since 1900 that today the Chinese greatly outnumber the Inner Mongols. In spite of this, the Chinese Communists, in accordance with a nationality policy modeled on that of the USSR (which preserves the form if not the substance of the minority culture), have designated Inner Mongolia, the Inner Mongolian Autonomous Region.

A careful study of Soviet and Chinese Communist maps of the Sino-Mongolian boundary prior to 1962 reveals a number of discrepancies, not all of which have apparent geographic significance. On Soviet maps, the boundary in the west proceeds southeastward from the Soviet frontier along the crest of the Mongolian Altay, but Chinese maps place the boundary considerably to the east. In effect, Chinese maps incorporate the Mongolian Altay into Sinkiang, thus securing control of the headwaters of a number of the rivers draining to the lowlands in Sinkiang. Other variations in the Sino-Mongolian boundary occur throughout the sparsely occupied Gobi to the east, as well as in the plateau region near the Siberian Trans-Baykal frontier. Many of these discrepancies also seem to have been to the disadvantage of the MPR.

In December, 1962, Premier Yunzhagin Tsedenbal of Mongolia reached an agreement with the Chinese Communists in Peking formally fixing their mutual boundary. However, the accord was soon followed by tension and vituperation, with the Mongols accusing the Chinese of trying to turn the republic into "an outlying region under Chinese power." This development may have prevented precise demarcation of the boundary.[9] At any rate, it is difficult to determine the extent to which changes in the boundary have occurred.

Unlike the Sino-Mongolian boundary, the Soviet-Mongolian boundary in modern times appears to be clearly marked. Much of it was determined by the 1727 Treaty of Kiakhta. Until 1944, the republic of Tannu-Tuva lay between northwestern Mongolia and Siberia, but in that year the Soviet Union annexed the territory, on the basis of a claim reaching back to Kiakhta. Tannu-Tuva had been detached from Outer Mongolia in the early 1920's and, though nominally independent, had been little more than a satellite of the USSR. Renamed the Tuvinian Autonomous Oblast, the region was thereafter made directly subordinate to Moscow. More recently, the oblast was reorganized as an autonomous republic. Native Tuvinians are a Turkic people.

For the most part, the Soviet-Mongolian boundary cuts across territory that, because of its difficult terrain, is sparsely occupied. From the Altay Mountains in the west to the plateau and ranges of Trans-Baykalia, the borderlands consist of one mountain mass after another, heavily wooded on the north face but dry and bare on the south.

Known as the Alps of Siberia, the Altay Mountains rise to about 10,000 feet. Because of their latitude, they receive fairly heavy precipitation throughout the year. Faulted and deeply dissected, the Altay have a rugged appearance, the grandeur of which is accentuated by the snow, which remains all year round on the higher peaks. In the Altay near the Mongolian border rise several of the headwater tributaries of the Ob, such as the Chuya, the Kamun, and the Biya.

Eastward, the Altay give way to the Sayan system, which from the air looks more like a deeply dissected plateau than a series of

---

[9] Ovdiyenko's study of contemporary Mongolia, published in 1964, shows no major change in the Sino-Mongolian boundary.

mountain ranges. The Soviet incorporation of Tannu-Tuva, an enclosed upland basin, placed the boundary to the south of the Tannu-Ola Range. This act resulted in a considerable shortening of the boundary and at the same time gave the USSR a natural advantage. Tannu-Tuva lies astride the shortest and easiest route between Western Siberia and Mongolia.

To the east, the Soviet-Mongolian boundary stretches across the ranges of the Eastern Sayan, which are higher than those of the Western Sayan. North of Lake Khobso Gol, the largest fresh-water lake in Mongolia, the boundary descends into a broad upland valley, which facilitates contact between north-central Mongolia and Irkutsk, the major city in Eastern Siberia. Eastward, the Dzhedinsk Range forms much of the boundary as far as the Selenga "crossing." The Selenga, the major river of Mongolia, drains northward into Lake Baykal, creating a natural route between Mongolia and Siberia. Not only does a motor road follow the valley, but a railway also enters Mongolia from the north, connecting Ulan-Ude on the Trans-Siberian to Ulan Bator, the capital of the MPR, and, ultimately, to Peking. The Mongolian Railway, opened in its entirety in 1956, thus affords the most direct rail link between Moscow and the Chinese capital.

East of the Selenga, the boundary rises into and crosses a series of relatively low ranges. To the east of the Onon River, the mountains give way to an extensive undulating plateau. Here, the boundaries of the USSR, the MPR, and the CPR meet. The shortest distance between Lake Baykal and Vladivostok on the Pacific is due east across Inner Mongolia and Manchuria, but the Sino-Soviet boundary, as we have already seen, follows the Argun northward to the Amur and around the hump of the Great Khingan.

In the Soviet territories immediately bordering Mongolia on the north, from Altay Kray to Chita Oblast, live approximately 10 million people (Table VI). Of these, some 500,000 belong to non-Slavic ethnic groups. In the Baykal area, mainly east of the lake, live approximately 270,000 Buryat Mongols. In the Tuvinian ASSR are close to 110,000 Tuvinians. To the west and north are other smaller Turkic-speaking groups, such as the Khakass (60,000) and the Altays (47,000). The rest of the population is essentially Russian, mixed with Ukrainian.

TABLE VI.

Population of the Siberian and Soviet Far Eastern Borderlands
(Jan. 1, 1965)

I.	Soviet Far East	5,427,000
	of which	
	Khabarovsk Kray	1,279,000
	(Jewish A.O.)	172,000
	Amur Oblast	769,000
	Maritime Kray	1,564,000
II.	Eastern Siberia	7,190,000
	of which	
	Krasnoyarsk Kray	2,901,000
	(Khakass A.O.)	458,000
	Tuvinian ASSR	207,000
	Irkutsk Oblast	2,227,000
	(Ust-Orda Buryat N.O.)	154,000
	Buryat ASSR	761,000
	Chita Oblast	1,094,000
III.	Western Siberia	10,843,000
	of which	
	Altay Kray	2,772,000
	(Gorno-Altay A.O.)	169,000
	Kemerovo Oblast	3,030,000

Source: *Narodnoye khozyaystvo SSSR v 1964. Statisticheskiy yezhegodnik,* Moscow, 1965, pp. 12–15.

During the Soviet period, the Siberian borderlands have undergone impressive industrialization. Between the Salair Range and the Kuznetsk Ala-Tau lies the Kuznetsk Basin, containing the largest deposits of high-quality coal in the USSR. Within the basin are seven cities, each with a population of over 100,000, the largest being Novokuznetsk, formerly Stalinsk, a metallurgical city (478,-000). Beyond the basin to the northwest lies the "primate city" of Siberia, Novosibirsk, with about 1,029,000 inhabitants. An administrative, industrial, and transportation city, Novosibirsk has become also the center of Soviet science in Siberia. Krasnoyarsk on the Yenisey has grown to over 541,000, while Irkutsk on the Angara is 401,000. The hydro developments on the Angara at Irkutsk and Bratsk and greater use of the nearby Cheremkhovo coal fields, as planned, should speed up the growth of the Baykal area. During the summer of 1961, the concrete dam at Bratsk, begun in 1955, was completed. When filled, its reservoir will create, according to Soviet claims, the largest man-made lake in the world, extending 350 miles upstream and reaching a width of 15 miles. The designed capacity of the Bratsk hydroelectric station is 4.5 million kilowatts. Meanwhile, the three-century old town of Bratsk has been submerged and the population relocated 20 miles downstream in a new city also known as Bratsk, which has grown to well over 140,000.

East of Lake Baykal, the population (partly Buryat) spreads out over the plateau, and the industrial cities of Ulan-Ude and Chita are both relatively small (213,000 and 198,000 respectively). From Novosibirsk to Chita, agriculture is restricted by the short growing season and, in many years, insufficient precipitation. The raising of livestock is the preferred activity of the Mongol and Turkic groups, but crop cultivation is also carried on, with grains predominating.

In spite of the growth of cities and the development of industry in the borderlands, Siberia still remains very much a frontier country. To the north for at least two thousand miles lie the relatively empty lands of the forest and tundra, an ever-present fact of geography that creates enormous problems and challenges.

In the years since the Communists gained control of China, Peking has steadily consolidated its position along the southern border of the Mongolian People's Republic, in the Inner Mongolian Autonomous Region in the east, an extension of the Kansu province northward to the international boundary in the center and in the Sinkiang-Uighur Autonomous Region in the far northwest.

Over the past sixty years there has been a gradual but steady movement of Chinese settlers into Inner Mongolia. This movement has been facilitated by the construction of railways, particularly in eastern Inner Mongolia, which is served by Southern Manchurian and Chinese railways and interconnecting lines. The short line northwestward from Peking, which since 1956 has afforded a direct route to Ulan Bator, has stimulated Chinese settlement beyond the Great Wall north and west of Kalgan, among the Chahar Mongols. Yet without irrigation, only extensive agriculture with heavy dependence on livestock is presently feasible over much of Inner Mongolia. This economy has been traditional of Inner Mongolia, contrasting with the intensive Chinese cultivation south of the Great Wall and with the nomadism of the Outer Mongols north of the Gobi. There are about 1.5 million Mongols in Inner Mongolia, but they have long been outnumbered by Chinese, by at least five to one. Industrial development will surely attract more Chinese. A full-cycle iron and steel plant has been constructed at the city of Paotow.

Modern Kansu province, bordering on the MPR to the west of the Inner Mongolian A.R., lies astride the historic route between China proper and the dry reaches of Inner Asia. To the north lie the arid wastes of the Gobi, to the south the towering Nan-Shan. Life along the Kansu Corridor is sustained by and centered in oases, traditionally guarded by the Great Wall from the attack of northern nomads. Through the corridor runs the railway which, but a few years back, was destined to connect with the Soviet Turk-Sib. The corridor, therefore, is a strategic one, whose importance has been further underlined by the discovery and exploitation of oil at Yumen, where reserves have been estimated at 500 million tons, one of the largest deposits in modern China. Because the corridor has permitted the flow of peoples and cultures from east to west throughout history, its population today is heterogeneous. In addition to Chinese, there are large minorities of Dungans (Chinese Muslims), Mongols (and Kalmyks), Turkic-speaking groups, and Tibetans.

The Historical Confrontation

I N view of the political vacuum that existed in central and northern Asia, reflected in the weakness of the native tribes and peoples, a 16th-century geopolitician might have come to the conclusion that Muscovy in the west and China in the east would one day find themselves with common frontiers. By mid-17th century he would have been confirmed in his prognostication and amazed, too, that so little time had been required for the event to come to pass. For the expansion of Russia into and across Siberia came with dramatic swiftness. Whatever the obstacles—resistance by this or that tribe, a difficult terrain in an inclement climate— they were quickly surmounted. But the force of that drive was rather abruptly halted when the Russians reached the outer limits of the Chinese realm. They would have had to summon additional men and supplies from the distant western citadel before the advance could continue. Moreover, the Russia of the Romanovs had reached the outer limits of the Celestial Empire, however vaguely defined, at a time when China, after a period of decline, had received a new organizational lift from the conquering Manchus.

Ancient China, the Middle Kingdom of the Yellow River Basin, had suffered through cycles of power and decline. In periods of its greatest glory, as during the Han Dynasty, 202 B.C.–A.D. 220, and again during the T'ang Dynasty, A.D. 618–906, the Chinese Empire had reached far out into Asia, including southern Manchuria, Mongolia, Turkestan, Tibet, and Indo-China. Later, during the Mongol period, 1260–1368, China south of the Great Wall was the richest part of the vast Mongol Empire, which extended across Asia right into the lands of the Rus. In the centuries that followed, however, China was plagued by internal disorders and attacks by outsiders. Finally, in 1644, invaders from Manchuria captured Peking and established the Manchu or Ch'ing Dynasty, giving China in the late 17th and early 18th centuries one of its greatest periods in modern history.

From the beginning, the confrontation of Russians and Chinese in Asia created tension—a tension that originated in the Amur Basin, quickly spread into the Mongolian plateau, and, by the middle of the 19th century, penetrated into Turkestan. While China remained strong, Russia could only probe gently. But in the 1840's, as European imperialism gathered momentum and the Manchu Dynasty first began to show signs of weakness, Russia prepared for a further expansion of her empire at the expense of her neighbor. As George Kennan recently pointed out,[1] once established in Asia, Russia was compelled from "sheer geopolitical necessity" to protect from foreign penetration and domination those areas which lie adjacent to Russian borders, namely, Manchuria, Outer Mongolia, and Sinkiang. Nor did her interest in the borderlands lessen with the collapse of the Chinese Empire in 1911 and her own revolutions of 1917. Although Bolshevik leaders made a great point of condemning tsarist imperialism, they were no less inclined to preserve whatever they could of the Russian position in Asia, in part because they feared Japan's militarism and in part because the Chinese Nationalists were unable to occupy effectively all of the traditional Chinese territories.

From the middle of the 17th to the middle of the 20th centuries, therefore, the ever-narrowing zone of contact between the Russian and Chinese Empires in Asia was one of tension and at times outright conflict.

[1] George F. Kennan, "Stalin and China," *The Atlantic Monthly*, May, 1961, p. 35.

SEVENTEENTH AND EIGHTEENTH CENTURIES

The Ural Mountains, the traditional boundary between Europe and Asia, have never constituted a significant barrier to general west-east movement. It was, for instance, only 30 years after Ivan IV had defeated the Volga remnants of the once powerful Mongol Horde and captured Kazan (1552) and Astrakhan (1556), that Slavic freebooters crossed into Sibir (Figure 3). Their venture was not part of the search for a "final frontier" for Muscovy, which had originated centuries before in the poorly drained, wooded lands of the Volga-Oka "mesopotamia" to the west. Rather, they were attracted by the wealth of furs and, perhaps, of precious metals which Siberia possessed.

A half-century later, after following the rivers and skirmishing with the weakly organized native tribes, the freebooters had established a string of fortified posts across the Vasyugan Plain, which was peremptorily annexed to the Russian state by the tsar. In swift succession the Russians built new posts to the east: Kuznetsk, 1618; Yeniseysk, 1619; Krasnoyarsk, 1628; Ilimsk, 1630; and Bratsk, 1631. Keeping well to the north of the open steppe and thereby avoiding contact with the numerous warlike tribes of Turkestan, the Russian drive across Siberia came up against little opposition until it reached Lake Baykal and the land of the Buryat Mongols, the most northerly of the Mongol peoples of East Asia.

With that the Russians turned north into the Lena Valley, where they founded Yakutsk in 1632. In 1639, overland, they reached the Sea of Okhotsk. The scattered, primitive tribes of eastern Siberia proved no match for the Russians, and in 1643 Poyarkov crossed the Stanovoy Mountains into the Amur Basin. Following the Zeya River to the Amur, he explored the latter to its mouth before turning northward to the Sea of Okhotsk. In 1649, Khabarov was despatched from Yakutsk to the Amur, or to Dauria, as the region was then called, to exact tribute in food and furs from the natives. He reached the upper Amur without difficulty, but the conquest of

Dauria proved not as simple a task. Khabarov sent back to Yakutsk for cannon, captured the village of Albasin, and moved aggressively down the Amur. These activities of the Russians ultimately provoked a clash with Manchu warriors, below the site of modern Khabarovsk.

Thus was set the stage for the conflict between the Russians and the Manchus, who since 1644 had been the rulers in Peking. During the Ming Dynasty (1368–1644), China had been compelled to withdraw for the most part south of the Great Wall. In the Ch'ing (Manchu) Dynasty, however, China had found a new energetic leadership which would, in the century following, not only restore the historic empire of the Han, but carry Mongol banners far beyond their previous extent (Figure 3).

For some 30 years, long after Khabarov's time, the Russians and Manchus clashed in the Amur Basin. During that period, the Russians subdued the Buryats and established additional fortified posts, which strengthened the line of communication west to Yeniseysk. Yet despite the founding of Nerchinsk (1656–58), Irkutsk (1661), Selenginsk (1665), and other posts, the line of supply was too long for an effective Russian posture along the Amur. After a series of skirmishes, the Manchu forces were able to halt the Russian drive, and the tension was resolved in the Treaty of Nerchinsk (1689). By that treaty, the Russians gained title to approximately 90,000 square miles of territory, although they were pushed back to the Stanovoy Mountains and prevented from navigating the Amur. The Russo-Chinese boundary thereafter followed the Argun River to its confluence with the Amur, thence along the Shilka to the Stanovoy. Eastward from the mountains to the Pacific, however, the boundary was never precisely delimited.

Although the Manchus surrendered to the Russians the title to northeastern Siberia, the Amur Basin for the next century and a half remained under the Manchus. Peter the Great might cherish the ambition of conquering all of the Far East right up to the Great Wall, and Catherine might recognize the value of the Amur as a route of supply to her possessions in Kamchatka, but the Russians were too weak in eastern Siberia to do anything about it.

According to Owen Lattimore, it was the alliance between the Manchus and the neighboring Eastern Mongols that had made the Manchu conquest of China possible in 1644 and had led to the strengthening of Chinese influence along the periphery. "The Manchu-Mongol alliances," he wrote, "built up a frontier power in Inner Mongolia, which protected the Manchu conquests in China; and it was only later, by using their position in Inner Mongolia as a fulcrum, that the Manchus extended their power into Outer Mongolia." [2] Indeed, it was the greatest of the Manchu emperors, K'ang Hsi (1662–1722), who succeeded in bringing under Chinese control the tribes of northern Manchuria, northern and western Mongolia, Turkestan, and Tibet.

Because of its nearness to the China plain, southern Manchuria, particularly the lands along the Liao and Han Rivers, had been ethnically Chinese since the 3rd century B.C. Central and northern Manchuria, however, had remained essentially the domain of the Manchus. Up to 1644, Manchu tribes, however, made periodic raids south of the Great Wall and reportedly carried back to Manchuria a million or more Chinese peasants. As a result of Russian pressure along the Amur, some of these Chinese were permitted to settle in the Manchurian plains. But from 1668 to 1673 the policy was reversed and Chinese colonists were forbidden to locate beyond Mukden. Even so, from time to time in the latter decades of the 17th century, an increasing number of Chinese were smuggled northward, providing the basis for ultimate Sinification.

The Russian advance into Baykalia and the establishment of a post at Irkutsk in 1661 created the possibility of serious Russo-Chinese rivalry in Mongolia. The Mongolian plateau had a strategic value for the Russians because one of the more direct routes to Peking lay across its rolling grasslands. In 1676, Spathary, the

[2] Owen Lattimore, *The Mongols of Manchuria,* New York: The John Day Company, 1934, p. 16.

leader of a tsarist mission to Peking, reported three possible routes into China from Russian territory. One was through Manchuria, but this route was closed later by the Treaty of Nerchinsk. Another followed the Irtysh River into and through northern Turkestan, but though it was a shorter route it was arduous because of the conflicts among the Mongol tribes living there. The third followed the natural corridor of the Selenga River south of Lake Baykal, past the Russian post at Selenginsk, which had been established in 1665. Via the tributaries, the Orkhon and Tola, the route proceeded southeast across the plateau to Peking. However, the Selenga route was difficult because of internecine Mongol conflicts.

During the century or more preceding 1676, after the passing of the great khans, the Mongol Empire had disintegrated into small independent tribal states. For some time the tribes of northern and western Mongolia had been at war. Possibly because some of the Western Mongols had been on relatively good terms with the Russians in Siberia—indeed, in 1628 some tribes, later known as Kalmyks, had migrated freely to the Volga, where they settled —the Northern Mongols requested the protection of the Manchu emperor, which they obtained in 1691. The Treaty of Kiakhta in 1727 permitted Russian traders to cross Mongolia. Also, by the treaty, Russia gained approximately 40,000 square miles of territory south of Lake Baykal between the Sayan Mountains and the Argun River. Northern or Outer Mongolia, as well as the lands to the south, or Inner Mongolia, remained clearly part of the emperor's domain. The boundary drawn through the Sayan was imprecise, however, and laid the basis for further Russian claims in this area.

In the early years of dominance, the Ch'ing emperors, who in effect acted as feudal overlords, favored the Outer Mongols, and thereby brought an element of stability to the plateau that it had not known for many generations. Nevertheless, Russian trade with China across Outer Mongolia never materialized. In the period from 1730 to 1850 there were few exchanges between the Russians and the Chinese in Mongolia.

Chinese contacts with the lands and peoples to the west of Mongolia, that is in Hsi-yu or the Western Region, are of ancient vintage. In 139 B.C., the Han Emperor Wu-ti sent a mission led by Chang Ch'ien to the Yueh-chih, a people who inhabited the Fergana Valley, in what is now Uzbekistan, to gain their support against Hsiung-nu, warlike tribes who lived in the region now embraced by Kansu, Ch'inghai and Sinkiang. Though the mission failed to elicit the aid of the Yueh-chih, the Chinese, nevertheless, launched a major attack on the Hsiung-nu in a strategic thrust designed to take complete control of Kansu. A short time later, the Chinese overran Fergana, establishing outposts even beyond. Thus, by 100 B.C. virtually all of the lands of Inner Asia to the west of China proper paid tribute to China. Only centuries later, with the emergence of a Western Turkic Confederation, was the vassal relationship broken. However, it was restored during the 7th century, and weakened again in subsequent centuries. Tibetans overran the region, and they were followed by Turkic tribes (Uighurs) migrating from the Mongolian plateau. Muslim Arabs from the west invaded Turkestan in the 10th century, and finally in the 13th century came the Mongol tribes under Genghis Khan. Despite the fluctuation of control, Chinese interest in Inner Asia remained alive for at least two reasons. In the first place, Chinese control of Sinkiang meant security against attack from the west; in the second, possession of the Kansu Corridor and its approaches insured control over the trade moving both toward the west and toward the east.

With the collapse of the Mongol Empire, which was followed by tribal conflicts, the Chinese were again able to extend their rule into Turkestan. By 1757, the Ch'ing emperor had smashed the power of the Western Mongols in Dzhungaria and overrun the oases of the Tarim. A new province was created: Dzhungaria and the Tarim Basin (Kashgaria) were united and called Sinkiang, "the new province."

In order to strengthen the defense of the western frontier of

Sinkiang, the Ch'ing government settled Sibos and other Manchurian tribes along the Ili. In 1760 about 10,000 Uighur families from the Tarim Basin were also settled in the valley. These people later were called Taranchais, or "agriculturalists," because, in contrast to the Kazakh and Mongol tribes who were nomadic, the Uighurs were sedentary peoples. In 1771 some Kalmyks who had settled along the Volga in the preceding century returned to their homeland.

In the decades that followed, Chinese control of Sinkiang was exercised mainly through the local chieftains and headmen, who were vassals of the emperor. Chinese policy was clearly one of divide and rule. There was little settlement from the Chinese provinces to the east, for the Chinese did not consider Sinkiang a desirable place to live. In a sense, Sinkiang was to them what Siberia was to the Russians. In 1757 the new dominion had been proclaimed a place of exile for criminals or political dissenters. Hence the only other Chinese in Sinkiang were those attached mainly to military garrisons and posts. They were transported there with their families, given land and seed, and encouraged to make themselves self-sufficient. Yet because the Chinese in Sinkiang were generally favored by tax concessions and other privileges, they were greatly resented by the native peoples.

Various native states west of Sinkiang in Western Turkestan, such as Kokand and Bokhara, and the Kazakh Hordes had recognized the suzerainty of the Ch'ing emperor. However, being so remote from China proper, they were never brought under direct control.

The Russians, meanwhile, halted in Mongolia and Manchuria by the strength of Ch'ing forces, continued active throughout the forests and grasslands of western Siberia, consolidating their hold on the upper reaches of the Yenisey, Ob, and Irtysh Rivers. Omsk, established in 1716, was followed by Semipalatinsk in 1718 and Barnaul in 1738 (Figure 5). Late in the 18th century, the Turkic tribes of the Altay Mountains came under Russian control, and the boundary of Outer Mongolia in the northwest was delimited. But there could be no direct Russo-Chinese exchange in Inner Asia so long as the Russians remained north of the pastures of the Kazakh nomads. It required almost another century of Russian expansion, this time into the dry steppe of the Semirechiye, before Russians and Chinese would meet in Turkestan.

NINETEENTH AND EARLY TWENTIETH CENTURIES

The century ending in 1789 marked the high point of China under the Ch'ing Dynasty. Thereafter, the empire's decline was sharp and perilous.

The tsarist government, aware of the increasing importance of its Pacific settlements, turned again to the problem of the Amur, which had been quiescent since 1689. Following the Opium War (1840–42), which demonstrated Ch'ing weakness, Russian pressure on the Amur again manifested itself. In 1846 an expedition was sent to explore the Amur, and in 1850, in violation of the Treaty of Nerchinsk, a Russian post was established at Nikolayevsk near the mouth. A Trans-Baykal army was organized and other posts were established, even on Sakhalin Island. The Russian advance, directed locally by the ambitious Nicholas Muraviev, Governor General of Eastern Siberia, took two directions: (a) eastward from Baykal and (b) southward along the coast from Okhotsk and Kamchatka. Unable to resist this new Russian pressure, the Chinese were compelled to negotiate.

In the Aigun Treaty of Friendship and Boundaries, ratified by both Russia and China in 1858, China ceded to Russia most of the territory north of the Amur, from the mouth of the Argun to the Pacific. Near the mouth of the Zeya, however, a small piece of territory, containing a number of Manchu villages, was left under the administration of the Ch'ing government. The treaty also provided for joint occupation of the territory east of the Ussuri to the Pacific (and south of the Amur), and for Russian and Manchu navigation of the Amur.

In short, by the terms of the treaty, the Russian Empire gained title to about 170,000 square miles of territory. Promptly, the Russians founded Khabarovsk, near the junction of the Amur and Ussuri.

Two years later, in the Treaty of Peking, the Russians forced another settlement on the Manchus, in which Russia took complete control of the territory east of the Ussuri, now known as the Maritime Kray, and further pared down Manchuria. In the meantime, the Russian Pacific naval base, which had first been established at Petropavlovsk on Kamchatka, and later moved to Nikolayevsk near the mouth of the Amur, was advanced in 1872 to Vladivostok, where the problem of winter ice was less severe.

The apparent collapse of Manchu China encouraged Russian expansion, essentially of an economic nature, in the Mongolian sector. A convention in 1860 between Russia and China established Russian trade with Outer Mongolia on an official basis. In the next year, a Russian consulate was opened near the Buddhist monastery at Urga, later Ulan Bator, and Russian merchants entered the Chinese dominion.

Far to the west, where the nomadic Kazakh tribes wandered over the steppe all the way from the Volga River to Dzhungaria, owing allegiance and paying tribute to the Ch'ing emperor, the Russian drive into the Inner Asian drylands also got underway. By the end of the 18th century, trade links had been established across Turkestan between Russia and China. At first this trade was carried on between the Russian inhabitants at Bukhtarma on the Irtysh and the natives at Tarbagatay (or Chuguchak) and Kuldja in Sinkiang. Later, other Russian centers, such as Semipalatinsk and Petropavlovsk, were involved. The Russians had the advantage of greater accessibility to Sinkiang than did the Chinese of the Central Provinces to the east. The journey by camel from Semipalatinsk to Tarbagatay and Kuldja took only two months one way; whereas, it took from 6 to 12 months to go from China proper to Kuldja. This factor obviously greatly affected Chinese control of the province, as the decades that followed clearly revealed.

In order to protect and expand their developing interest in Turkestan, the Russians decided on military conquest of the native peoples of the area. They employed a two-pronged offensive (Figure 5) southeastward from the Urals to the Syr-Darya and the borders of the Khanates of Khiva and Bokhara. Persistently, the expeditions of the tsar pushed deeper into the lands nominally under the over-lordship of the Chinese emperor, moving from one advance position to another, consolidating as they went. By 1854, they had penetrated southeast of Lake Balkhash, into the lower Ili Valley, one of the main routes into Sinkiang. North of Lake Issyk-Kul in the foothills of the Tien-Shan they founded the town of Vernyi (now Alma-Ata). The Kuldja Convention of 1851 gave Russia greater freedom of trade at Kuldja on the upper Ili and at Tarbagatay. Now they were ready to compel the Chinese to come to terms on a boundary between their respective empires which would above all recognize the Russian conquests.

The Treaty of Peking, which determined the Ussuri River boundary in the Far East, also began the process of delimitation of the Sino-Russian boundary in Inner Asia. Four years later, in an agreement signed at Tarbagatay, the boundary was established from Mongolia southwestward to the limits of the Khanate of Kokand. Although many points were left vague and undefined, title to the Tien-Shan region south of Lake Issyk-Kul passed to Russia. In 1868, the Russian steppe province of Semipalatinsk, bordering on Sinkiang, augmented by the addition of former Chinese territory, was reorganized as Turkestan Oblast. Finally, in 1870, the Boundary Treaty of Uliassutay completed the delimination of the Inner Asian boundary, particularly where Mongolia, Sinkiang and Siberia meet.

Because of its remoteness, a factor referred to above, Sinkiang was a difficult province to control effectively from Peking. Indeed, since the Turkic-speaking peoples had not reconciled themselves to Chinese domination, the vast territory was periodically torn by armed uprisings. These revolts, usually very bloody, were aimed more or less at driving the Chinese from Sinkiang and at separating Sinkiang from the Chinese Empire. There were insurrections in

1825–26, 1827, 1830, 1857, and finally in 1864. The last revolt began in Dzhungaria, involving both Turks and Dungans, who soon succeeded in throwing off the Manchu yoke. In this effort, they were assisted by the Chinese garrisons in Sinkiang, which were also composed mainly of Dungans.

While this revolt was occurring north of the Tien-Shan, another uprising occurred in the Tarim Basin. The rebels sought the assistance of Yakub, a Kokandian general in Andijan to the west. He marched an army into Sinkiang and occupied the Tarim oases. Moving north, he defeated the leaders of the Dzhungarian revolt and occupied Urumchi. Yakub proclaimed himself Beg of a separate state, which received limited support form both Britain and Turkey. Britain was not unwilling to see a buffer state established between the Russian positions in Turkestan and her own empire in India. However, the separate state survived only until 1877, when Yakub Beg was reported to have committed suicide.

The British support for the revolt in Sinkiang encouraged the Russians to act. In 1871, a Russian military force crossed the frontier, ostensibly to keep order, and occupied the upper Ili district, including Kuldja (Figure 5). At the same time, the Russians attempted to extract from Peking the cession of the valley of the tributary Tekes River, along with strategic passes through the bordering ranges. The Chinese, however, refused to comply with the demands of the Russians and threatened war. The Russians, therefore, remained at Kuldja only until the Chinese, supported diplomatically by the European powers who had no desire to see a complete collapse of the Ch'ing Empire, were able to muster the strength to overcome the dissident Muslims. The Treaty of St. Petersburg in 1881 reaffirmed Chinese possession of the upper Ili, and the Russians agreed to relinquish their conquest, upon payment of an indemnity by China of nine million rubles. In addition, however, Russia obtained title to 18,000 square miles of territory near Lake Zaysan. That the Russian presence was not unwelcome in the Ili region by at least some of the native population is evidenced by the fact that when the Russians withdrew, thousands of Dungans and Uighurs followed the tsarist army into Russian territory. Under the terms of the treaty, the Chinese ceded a small area west of the Holkuts River to Russia, for the purpose of settling the emigrants there. Most of the Dungans settled near the Chinese border, although some went westward to the Fergana Valley.

In spite of the success in subduing the Muslims, Chinese control over Sinkiang remained perilously weak in the decades that followed, even though it had been made a regular province of the empire in 1884.

Thus Russia, in spite of having been defeated in the Crimean War, was on the move all across Asia. With its political power weakening, the Ch'ing Dynasty could offer little opposition. The only effective way it could prevent the loss of the borderlands to Russia was to make them unquestionably Chinese. In the last decades of the 19th century, therefore, colonization became a vital goal of imperial Chinese state policy.

Hitherto, as noted above, the Ch'ing emperors had forbidden Chinese settlement in the central and northern part of Manchuria. Between 1750 and 1806, a series of edicts renewed the prohibition, although the policy was somewhat relaxed in 1803. However, the restriction against Chinese migration was difficult to enforce, and it therefore proved ineffective. It was not possible to preserve the Manchu patrimony. Chinese infiltration continued and, following the cession of the territory beyond the Amur to Russia in 1858–60, began to intensify. In 1860–61, settlers began moving onto the virgin plains north of Harbin and northwest of Kirin. By 1878, there were more than 100,000 Chinese households north of Harbin. In that year, the Manchus gave their official blessing to the Sinification of the territory.

Chinese settlement in Inner and Outer Mongolia was slower to develop, partly because the aridity compelled a major adjustment in traditional Chinese agricultural practices. Nevertheless, as the

Trans-Siberian Railway was extended across Siberia to Lake Baykal and Russian settlers found their way into Urianghay and Buryatia, the Ch'ing government countered with projects to establish agricultural communities in the river valleys of northern and central Outer Mongolia.

The first plans for a Trans-Siberian Railway had been proposed in 1855, partly to afford an outlet to European Russia for the grain of western Siberia. Moreover, if Russia was to play a dominant role in Asia, a railway linking its far-flung possessions would have to be built. In 1891, work began on the section from Vladivostok to Khabarovsk on the Amur. From 1892–95 construction proceeded eastward from Chelyabinsk in the Urals to Lake Baykal.

The strengthening of the Russian position in Asia, and especially in the Far East, was dictated also by fear of Japanese intentions. Indeed, though Russia took advantage of the opportunities presented by the waning power of the Ch'ing government to expand at China's expense, she also realized that China offered a counterpoise to Japan. This was demonstrated in 1895 when, having defeated China in a brief war, Japan imposed a treaty that would have quickened the collapse of the Ch'ing government. In addition to the Pescadores and Formosa, Japan was ready to seize the Liaotung Peninsula in southern Manchuria with its strategic Port Arthur. Only the combined intervention of Russia, Germany, and France compelled Japan to modify her demands. After the war, in exchange for loans and guarantees of friendship, Russia secured from China permission to construct a railway across Manchuria that would link Lake Baykal with Vladivostok. Such a line would cut 340 miles off an all-Russian route along the Amur. At the same time, the railway would facilitate the spread of Russian economic, military and political influence throughout Manchuria and North China. When the Germans occupied Kiaochow Bay across the Yellow Sea from Liaotung in 1897, Russia obtained mining rights in southern Manchuria, leases to Port Arthur and nearby Dairen, and permission to extend the railway from Harbin to Dairen. Thus, while posing as China's friend, Russia secured what Japan had won by war but had been subsequently deprived of.

The Boxer Rebellion of 1900 reflected Chinese frustration and resentment over the course of events. Immediately, however, Russia brought Manchuria under military control. Chinese and Manchu villagers on the left bank of the Amur near the mouth of the Zeya, who had remained under Manchu administration after 1858, were driven out, and the region was annexed. After the rebellion had subsided, Russia was compelled to retreat to the position she had held in Manchuria before 1900, although the villages were not restored.

In view of the nature of both Russian and Japanese ambitions in China, conflict was probably unavoidable between the two powers. Japan watched the Russian advance in Manchuria with steadily increasing concern. When in 1904–05 Russian interest manifested itself in the guise of lumber concessions along the Yalu River in northern Korea, which had come largely within the Japanese sphere after 1895, war resulted.

Though having taken an aggressive role in the Far East, Russia was nevertheless ill-prepared to support her policy successfully. Unable to supply the Far Eastern forces and disrupted by revolution, the Russian war effort came to an abrupt end. Not only did Russia surrender to Japan the South Manchurian Railway and Port Arthur, together with access to the mineral resources of southern Manchuria, but also title to the southern half of Sakhalin. Sakhalin had become legally Russian by a treaty in 1875 which had also conceded Japan title to the Kurile Islands to the northeast. In the détente that followed in 1907 (and ultimately made Russia and Japan allies of the United Kingdom and France in World War I), Russia and Japan agreed on separate spheres of influence in China. Although Chinese sovereignty over Manchuria was affirmed, Russia recognized Japan's pre-eminent position in the south and in Inner Mongolia to the east. In return, Russian influence was recognized as paramount in northern Manchuria, Outer Mongolia, and Sinkiang. In effect, therefore, the Russian sphere contained practically all of the territory north of what later came to be called the Kuropatkin Line. Named after General Kuropatkin, the line was drawn by political strategists in St. Petersburg along the 43rd parallel, eastward from the Khan-Tengri Range in the Tien-Shan to Vladivostok, as a possible boundary between Russia and China in Asia.

The Sino-Japanese War and the Russo-Japanese War, both of which concerned Chinese territory, made colonization of Manchuria even more urgent from the Chinese point of view. In 1908, Chinese governmental administration was imposed on the region, and all legal bans on settlement were lifted. Ironically, the Russian-built railways facilitated the Chinese peasant movement northward. The population of Manchuria thereafter increased rapidly.

After the turn of the century, Chinese peasant migration into eastern Inner Mongolia also increased, and large-scale, systematic colonization began in Outer Mongolia. In 1908, Peking reinforced its garrison in Urga and began intensive colonization along the Kalgan-Urga caravan route through the Gobi. In 1911, the year the Ch'ing government was overthrown, a Chinese colonization bureau was opened in Urga to expedite the movement northward. The increasing presence of the Chinese peasant farmer in Mongolia did much to fire Mongol nationalism, already provoked by Chinese economic exploitation and the shrewdness of the Chinese merchants. These developments in Mongolia did not go unnoticed in St. Petersburg.

The reforms planned by China in Mongolia—Chinese tillers to colonize the strips of land bordering us, the linking of the same by railways, at points which would be close to this frontier, with Chinese administrative centers and the distribution of Chinese troops, especially the appearance of considerable Chinese armed forces in the close neighborhood of our possessions, cannot fail to disturb us [it was stated at conference on foreign affairs in St. Petersburg in 1911]. Therefore, the Mongolian question is for us of great importance, and our support of the Mongols in their aspiration to counteract the above-mentioned undertaking of the Chinese government would fully correspond with our interests.[3]

Early in 1911, the Outer Mongols petitioned the Russian tsar for aid in throwing off the Chinese yoke. The Russians supplied arms and promised assistance, while the collapse of the Ch'ing Dynasty in Peking created the opportunity for intervention.

The revolution in Peking and the establishment of a Chinese Republic made evident at once, according to Owen Lattimore, the old cleavages between Outer and Inner Mongolia. Revolutionary movements had actually begun earlier in Inner Mongolia than in Outer Mongolia, but had never made much headway. Proximity to the North China Plain had given the economy of the Inner Mongols quite a different character from that of their nomadic cousins north of the Gobi; Chinese colonization further enhanced this difference. Among Outer Mongols, however, anti-Ch'ing sentiment was widespread.

Late in 1911, Outer Mongolia proclaimed its independence, but such a development was not desired by Russia. In 1913, therefore, Russia, serving as mediator, forced the Mongols to recognize Chinese suzerainty. Two years later, the future role of Outer Mongolia became clearer when, in the Kiakhta Agreement, the province was made a buffer between Russia and China. Outer Mongolian autonomy within the Chinese Empire was reaffirmed, but Russia secured the right of free trade in the territory. What this meant was that despite Chinese suzerainty, Outer Mongolia had in effect become a Russian protectorate. But not for long. Following the revolutionary upheaval in Russia, the President of China, in November, 1919, proclaimed the cancellation of Outer Monoglian autonomy, and Chinese troops crossed the Gobi.

Republican China, however, was no more welcome in Outer Mongolia than Imperial China had been in its last years. In 1918, a People's Revolutionary Party had been formed in Mongolia, and

[3] Peter S. H. Tang, *Russian and Soviet Policy in Manchuria and Outer Mongolia, 1911–1931,* Durham: Duke University Press, 1959, p. 297.

in March, 1921, a provisional government had been proclaimed at Kiakhta, on Russian territory. Several months later, Red Army troops from Lake Baykal entered Urga.

In 1911 while attempting to gain control of Outer Mongolia as a whole, Tsarist Russia had occupied and detached from Outer Mongolia its northwestern province, Urianghay. In 1914, a Russian protectorate was proclaimed over it. But with the revolution in Russia, Urianghay again came under Mongol or Chinese jurisdiction, only to have Soviet authority reestablished in 1918. In 1921, Urianghay "proclaimed" itself an independent republic called Tannu-Tuva, but is was clearly a Soviet satellite.

In Sinkiang, to the west, the Russian penetration after 1881 was largely of an economic nature. Following the annexation of the borderlands, especially east of Lake Balkhash in the Semirechiye, a series of Cossack settlements had been established. Imposed on the fertile grasslands of the Kazakh nomads, these settlements involved from 12,000 to 15,000 people, who were followed soon after by Russian peasant colonists. The inroads of the crop cultivators were sorely resented by the pastoralists. Nevertheless, as far as the tsarist government was concerned, Semirechiye was important because it faced the most dangerous spot for Russia in Asia. Here were the corridors of Inner Asia. The settlements were designed to secure the Russian position against the nomad and afford at the same time a buffer along the Chinese flank.

Decades later, in the middle of World War I, the corridors continued to have an effect on geopolitical thinking in Russia. Indeed, as far as General A. N. Kuropatkin, who became Governor General of Turkestan in 1916, was concerned,

. . . the future danger for Russia from this empire of 400,000,000 people is beyond all doubt. The most vulnerable part of the Russian frontier, as 800 years ago, remains that great gateway through which the hordes of Genghis Khan poured into Europe. So long as Kuldja (i.e., on the Ili) rests in the hands of the Chinese, the protection of Turkestan from

China will remain very difficult, or will demand a great number of troops. This gateway must not be left in the hands of the Chinese. A change in our boundary with China is urgently necessary.[4]

Thus, Kuropatkin would adopt a boundary that gave Russia all of mainland Asia north of the 43rd parallel—including Kuldja!

The Semirechiye settlements enjoyed considerable success. In 1912, the tsarist government granted a charter for a railway to a Semirechiye company to further the economic development of the area and to facilitate further colonization. In 1911, the construction of the railway south from Novosibirsk on the Trans-Siberian began, but the road reached only to Semipalatinsk when the First World War broke out.

The resentment of the Kazakh nomads, whose best grasslands had been occupied and their nomad routes of migration from summer to winter pastures had been cut, led to bloody uprisings against the Russians in mid-summer 1916. It was the seriousness of this situation that had led to the appointment of Kuropatkin as governor general. Some Kazakhs continued to fight on against the Imperial Russians; others joined the Bolsheviks, hoping that the success of the latter would benefit their own cause. At any rate, the Bolshevik Revolution of 1917 would have repercussions for all the native peoples of Russian Turkestan.

1917–1945

In the period immeditely following the Bolshevik Revolution, the Soviet leaders were inclined to disassociate themselves from tsarist imperial policies. In particular, they denounced the treaties that had been imposed on China and condemned tsarist hegemony in the borderlands. Pledges were made to the future equality of Sino-Soviet relationships. Moreover, shortly after the seizure of power, the Soviet leaders promised to transfer to Republican China

[4] Richard A. Pierce, *Russian Central Asia, 1867–1917,* Berkeley and Los Angeles: University of California Press, 1960, p. 298.

the Chinese Eastern Railway, which had been built by Russia and maintained as a Russian state possession.

The collapse of civil government in Russia, however, encouraged the Japanese to intervene on the mainland. On April 5, 1918, Japanese troops landed at and occupied Vladivostok, on the pretext of protecting Japanese lives and property. They seized the Chinese Eastern Railway and advanced along the Trans-Siberian as far as Chita. In the meantime, Czech troops, who had been captured by the Russians during the World War, began moving eastward along the Trans-Siberian toward their destination, the port of Vladivostok. There they hoped to be removed by the Allies and transported to the western front against Germany. By June, 1918, the anti-Communist Czechs had sealed off western Siberia from Moscow. Also various anti-Communist Russian "governments" were established from time to time across the vast stretch of Siberia, but it proved impossible to create a single anti-Bolshevik authority to coordinate or unite their activities.

Throughout 1919, the situation gradually worsened for the Bolshevik opposition in Siberia. The Czech legion was finally evacuated, leaving the Bolshevik forces advancing from the west, while the Japanese troops east of Lake Baykal remained the only effective force in Siberia. Under these circumstances, an attempt was made, with Japanese encouragement, to establish a buffer state in eastern Siberia. The Far East Republic, which came into existence in April, 1920, was a compromise. It was neither Bolshevik nor reactionary, but proclaimed itself "independent democratic." In May, the Soviet government recognized it.

Since the Far East Republic had pledged itself not to admit Soviet Russian armies to its territory, the Japanese withdrew their troops to the Maritime region. But, by skillful diplomacy, Japan was outmaneuvered. The republic did not take on the characteristics of a buffer. Finally, primarily as a result of pressure from the English-speaking powers, Japan was compelled to withdraw entirely from the mainland. By November, 1922, her troops were back in Japan;

the Maritime region was incorporated into the Far East Republic; and on November 10, 1922, the republic voted itself into the Russian Soviet Federated Socialist Republic, ceasing to exist as a separate entity. Within the year, a Buryat-Mongol ASSR was established on the shores of Lake Baykal, to accommodate the Mongols of Eastern Siberia.

Thus by 1923 Soviet authority was established throughout Siberia. The withdrawal of the Japanese also gave the Russians possession once again of the Chinese Eastern Railway. But the Soviets did not redeem the promise that they had made earlier, to return the railway to China—primarily because of their fear of and concern over Japanese Far Eastern ambitions. But when the Soviets were finally compelled to sell the railway, it was not to China—but to Japan! The transfer (in 1935) was a recognition of a changed power situation, for in 1931 Japan had invaded Manchuria and subsequently established the puppet state of Manchukuo.

In a treaty with China in 1915, Japan had secured 99-year leases on Port Arthur and Dairen, as well as on the South Manchurian Railway. In the years that followed, Japan increasingly dominated the economic life of Manchuria, while leaving the local administration in the hands of Chinese separatist leaders. In the latter 1920's, conflicts between the separatists in Manchuria and the Chinese Kuomintang (or Chinese Nationalists) brought increased tension. Finally, in order to prevent the Chinese Nationalists from gaining control of Manchuria, the Japanese decided to take over the entire province. In the years that followed, from 1933 to 1945, Japan implemented a program of development that resulted in the creation of the southern Manchurian industrial base, the so-called "Far Eastern Ruhr."

Soviet strength throughout the period from the revolution to the Second World War was not sufficient to dislodge the Japanese from their position of paramountcy in Manchukuo and North China, however ardently the Russians might desire it. Instead, the Soviet Far Eastern territories had to be strengthened and protected, if possible without resort to armed conflict. This task was made all the more urgent during the middle and late 1930's as Nazi Germany's militarism posed a threat in Europe to the western borderlands of the Soviet Union. Consequently, the Soviet regime decided to construct a second Siberian railway, which would parallel the main route but run at some distance to the north of the Mongolian-Manchurian border. Known as the Baykal-Amur Railway, it was to link Tayshet on the Trans-Siberian northwest of Irkutsk with the new port of Sovetskaya Gavan on the Pacific, almost due east of Komsomolsk. Although construction got underway before World War II, only short sections of the railway were completed by 1941, so it contributed little if anything to Soviet defenses in the Far East. After the war, it was reported that Japanese prisoners of war were put to work on the railway, but there are no known reliable data to indicate that the Baykal-Amur has ever been finished.

The autonomous position of Outer Mongolia within the Chinese Empire had been agreed upon by Russia, China, and Outer Mongolia in 1915. Real power in Outer Mongolia, however, lay with the Russians—at least until 1917. For a brief period following the Bolshevik Revolution, it seemed that Russia would not regain her hegemony over Outer Mongolia. But the short-lived rule of Chinese and White Russians in Outer Mongolia revealed to the new Bolshevik regime in Moscow how easily the territory might serve as a springboard for attack on the vital Trans-Siberian Railway. Furthermore, Outer Mongolia in any other hands but Soviet Russian might prove a source of disaffection for the Buryat Mongols to the north. In 1921, therefore, the Red Army occupied Urga; in 1924 the Mongolian People's Republic, with a constitution modelled on that of the Russian Republic, came officially into being. In reality, the territory was little more than a Soviet satellite, even though the Russians still claimed to recognize Chinese suzerainty over Outer Mongolia. These developments did not occur without strong protests from China, but there was little that the Chinese Republic could do. For nearly thirty years thereafter the Soviet hold on the Mongolian

Republic remained unshakable. The MPR was cut off and isolated from the rest of the world.

As has been mentioned before, nomadic livestock herding had been the traditional occupation of the Outer Mongols for centuries. Before 1921, and particularly before 1911, whatever cultivation of the soil there was—and acreage was not large due, in part, to the unfavorable climate—was mostly carried on by Chinese peasant settlers. The Mongol preferred his way of life and despised those who made a living working the soil. With the exodus of most of the remaining Chinese from Mongolia after the Communist Revolution of 1921, the new Mongol regime attempted to settle its nomads. In 1929–30, it made an effort to collectivize the agricultural economy of the country, but the movement ended in complete failure. The opposition of the nomads to surrendering their vast herds led to the slaughtering of large numbers of animals. Some drove their sheep and goats over the border into Inner Mongolia to escape collectivization. Few livestock cooperatives survived. At the same time, the regime (in the First Mongolian Five-Year Plan introduced in 1930) directed that the sown area be raised to over 240,000 acres. But, this effort, too, brought little success, for as late as 1940 there were no more than 65,000 acres under cultivation in Mongolia.

These efforts to alter drastically the economy of the country must be visualized against a background of state oppression and international tension. The regime waged a systematic campaign against the traditional Mongol social system. Large numbers of Buddhist monks were purged and most of the monasteries were closed. Some monasteries were completely destroyed, their treasures carried away. A new elite was trained in the image created by Moscow. As World War II approached, the Soviets were unquestionably concerned about Mongolia. In 1936, a Soviet-Mongolian defensive alliance, aimed at Japan, proclaimed that the USSR would defend the MPR as if it were Soviet territory. Indeed, plans had reportedly been made in Moscow for the annexation of the MPR by the USSR. At any rate, the Soviets possibly realized that a Japanese attack on Mongolia might very well gain the support of the Mongol people as a whole.

With respect to Tannu-Tuva, neither the Mongolians nor the Tuvinians had sought the separation that the Soviets had imposed on them, but in a gesture of conciliation to the Mongols the Russians transferred Darkhat, a small, sparsely inhabited strip west of Lake Khobso Gol, to the MPR (Figure 6). In 1927, less than a fifth of the population of Tannu-Tuva were Russians. In the decades that followed, as a result of systematic colonization, the complexion of the population changed substantially to the disadvantage of the native Tuvinians. Clearly, the Soviet leaders were intent on keeping Tannu-Tuva and the MPR apart. Finally, in October, 1944, Tannu-Tuva was secretly annexed to the USSR, an event which the rest of the world did not discover until some months later. Reorganized as the Tuvinian Autonomous Oblast directly subordinate to Moscow, the mountain basin was given a unique status in the Soviet political-administrative hierarchy. [The territory has since been reorganized as the Tuvinian ASSR.]

On the eve of World War I, according to Louis Fischer, Russia had also seriously intended to annex Dzhungaria, the northern half of Sinkiang province. To seek to annex the Tarim Basin to the south would antagonize Great Britain because of the special interest which the Tarim Basin held for British India.[5] Any such move was forestalled however by the war and revolution. The chaos in Russia, coupled with the difficulties facing the Kuomintang in China proper, allowed Sinkiang to live for several years as a semi-independent state under its Chinese governor.

Because the Bolsheviks were already threatening to disrupt their traditional nomadic way of life, 100,000 Kazakhs sought asylum in Sinkiang shortly after the revolution. However, the migration of the Kazakhs soon came to a halt when the Russian Communists, under Lenin's leadership, altered their tactics and sought to pose

[5] Louis Fischer, *The Soviets in World Affairs,* Princeton: Princeton University Press, 1951, Vol. II, p. 534.

as champions of the smaller ethnic groups, including the Turkic peoples of Central Asia.

This change of policy was used to further Soviet penetration of Sinkiang. The Ili Provisional Trade Agreement of 1920, between the Soviet Union and the governor of Sinkiang, Yang Tseng-hsin, had restricted Soviet Russian trading activities to Ili. Several years later, however, as Soviet authority was imposed on Central Asia, Russian interest in the affairs of Sinkiang quickened. An agreement in 1924 with the new governor of Sinkiang, Chen Shu-jen, who came increasingly to depend on Soviet aid to maintain his own position, made possible wider Soviet trade in Sinkiang. The Soviets, moreover, were permitted to establish consulates at Altay (Sharashune), Chuguchak (Tarbagatay), Kuldja, Kashgar, and Urumchi. They opened theaters and libraries, which quickly became centers of Communist propaganda. By the end of the decade, the whole of Sinkiang's foreign trade was in Soviet hands. The completion in 1930 of the Turkestan-Siberian Railway, south from Semipalatinsk to Alma-Ata, assisted materially the Soviet economic offensive in Sinkiang.

The relative calm that had prevailed throughout Sinkiang in the 1920's came to an end in 1931. That year, when Japan invaded Manchuria, was equally critical for Sinkiang. Not only did a mass migration of thousands of Chinese into the province from the east occur, but the native Dungans revolted against the local Chinese administration. Though resembling Chinese, the Dungans nevertheless had a different way of life, based in part on their belief in Islam. The Chinese governor was unable to bring the revolt under control and was compelled to accept Soviet assistance. In return, in a secret agreement—later declared void by the Chinese Nationalist Government but with little effect—he removed all trade restrictions against the Soviet Union. Through the Soviet-Sinkiang Trading Agency, Soviet Russia gained complete control over the commerce and economy of Sinkiang.

Shortly thereafter, another armed uprising occurred in the oases of the Tarim Basin, this time led by Turkic-speaking Muslims, who, tacitly supported by the British, proclaimed at Kashgar a Muslim Republic of East Turkestan. Turkic forces laid siege to Urumchi. The new Chinese governor, General Sheng Shih-ts'ai, was compelled to seek Russian assistance, which led ultimately to the defeat of the rebels in July, 1934. Such was the ethnocentrism of the native peoples of Sinkiang that, in spite of their Islamic faith, they were unable to make common cause against the much-disliked Chinese overlords.

In the meantime, the political situation in Sinkiang was further complicated by events in adjacent Kazakhstan. When Stalin began his drive for all-out collectivization, at least 250,000 Kazakhs moved south and east with their herds and flocks. Some went on over the mountains into India. Others attempted to settle in Chinese territory. Yet in spite of the activities of the Russian Communists, the Kazakhs probably still regarded the Chinese as traditional enemies. Their arrival in Sinkiang was not, therefore, a stabilizing event.

In order to secure Soviet military assistance in putting down the Turkic revolt, Governor Sheng, who was a professed Communist, politically oriented toward the Soviet Union, agreed to major concessions. Without obtaining the consent of the Nationalist Government in Nanking, he surrendered (to the Soviets) in return for a loan of five million rubles a monopoly of the province's exports of raw materials. Hence, from 1932 to 1943, when the Russians were compelled to withdraw, Sinkiang was little more than a Soviet satellite. Red Army garrisons were much in evidence not only in Hami in eastern Dzhungaria but throughout the province.

During that period the Russians built up a large network of Communist institutions, headed by Soviet advisers, who crossed the border in the guise of specialists or even anti-Bolshevik *emigres*. At the same time the Soviets made strong efforts to awaken the national consciousness of the peoples of Sinkiang, in order to use them against the Chinese Nationalists. In this connection, to propagandize the natives, well-indoctrinated Turkestanis were sent in from Soviet Central Asia. The Chinese Kazakhs, like the other peoples, for the most part took the overtures of friendship by the Russians at their face value, in spite of what they might have learned from the Russian Kazakhs. Thus, the events from 1931 to 1934 tended to stimulate on the the one hand Pan-Turkist feeling and, on the other, Uighur and Kazakh nationalism, further weakening earlier Pan-Islamist ties.

Domination of Sinkiang's commerce had been a major objective of Soviet policy. Of even greater importance to the Soviets was complete control over the exploitation of Sinkiang's mineral wealth. In 1934 Soviet geologists began surveying the province and preparing maps of its resources. The Soviets were particularly interested in finding oil, but Sinkiang's output of tungsten enabled the Soviets to cut back on imports from other parts of China.

Governor Sheng's policies and increasing Soviet penetration of all aspects of life in Sinkiang led to a revolt in 1936. But the uprising failed. Thousands were massacred, and others fled eastward into Kansu, pursued by the Red Army. In 1937, another popular revolt broke out in Yarkend, aimed at driving both the Russians and the Chinese out. Russian troops helped put down the revolt, but again the bloodshed was considerable. These revolts in no way weakened Soviet influence in, or control of, Sinkiang. If anything, the military occupation grew. In 1940, a lend-lease agreement between Governor Sheng and the Soviets gave the latter additional privileges in the province, including the right to explore for zinc and other minerals, to construct a communications network, and to send additional troops to guard various Soviet installations.

In 1940 still another revolt broke out in Sinkiang, this time in Altay province among the Kazakhs. Because the northwest possesses tne richest mineral deposits in Sinkiang, the region was of special interest to the Russians. Yet, despite the efforts of both the Russians and Governor Sheng, the revolt continued for several years.

Meanwhile, the outbreak of World War II was about to have a very important influence on events in Sinkiang. In June, 1941, the

Nazis invaded the USSR, while in the following December the Japanese attacked Pearl Harbor, bringing the USA into the conflict. Governor Sheng suddenly turned against his Soviet "advisers" and sought an understanding with Chiang Kai-shek, at this time allied with and supported by the USA in the common fight against Japan. Sheng's abrupt about-face, along with the disorders in the Altay region, weakened the Soviet position in Sinkiang. Finally, beginning in 1942 as a result of German pressure in the west, the Soviets were forced to withdraw their forces from Sinkiang. Kuomintang troops were dispatched to put down the native uprisings and Governor Sheng was replaced. The year 1943, therefore, marks the beginning of direct Chinese Nationalist rule in Sinkiang in any real sense, but the period thereafter was too brief and difficult a time for effective control to be imposed.

There was no reason why the native peoples of Sinkiang should welcome the Kuomintang. Before his removal Governor Sheng had begun to implement a policy toward the nationalities which he hoped would find favor with Chiang Kai-shek. This policy reflected the "Greater Chinese Theory," subscribed to by Chiang, according to which the nationalities of China were all one nation and one race; that is to say, Chinese. Thus, whereas before Sheng had permitted Soviet encouragement of local feeling, he now began to suppress local nationalisms. With the resident Communists, he was even more ruthless. Indeed, he is reported to have eliminated all Chinese Communists in Sinkiang in 1942, including Mao Tse-tung's brother. But Sheng's sudden embrace of the Nationalist cause could not keep him in office. Although his successor announced that he had come to bring local autonomy to all, few were convinced, and the native uprisings continued.

From 1943 on, the situation in Sinkiang was one of considerable confusion. The anti-Chinese revolt which flared up at Kuldja (Ining) in November, 1944, was aided by the Soviets. Well-armed and equipped, the rebel forces drove the Chinese Nationalist troops out of northwestern Sinkiang, winning a major victory at Wusu in the summer of 1945. Immediately, a Revolutionary Republic of Eastern Turkestan was proclaimed. The Soviets offered to mediate the dispute, and the rebels, on the verge of capturing Urumchi, surprisingly acquiesced. Obviously, the Russians were calling the tune.

The efforts to establish effective Kuomintang administration in China while carrying on a struggle with the Chinese Communists elsewhere would not permit Chiang Kai-shek to deploy sufficient resources to remote Sinkiang. The appointment of Governor Chang Chih-chung in 1945 to bring peace to Sinkiang and to improve relations with the Soviet Union had little positive effect. Time had run out. It would be, as we shall see, only a matter of weeks after major Communist victories in the east that Sinkiang would fall into Chinese Communist hands in the west.

3 *Sino-Soviet Relations and the Communist Revolution*

THE PERIOD OF 1945-49

Iт was generally believed in the United States, after Germany's defeat in World War II seemed apparent, that the war with Japan in the Far East would go on for many months after the cessation of European hostilities. The prolongation of the war, too, it was acknowledged, would cost the lives of many Americans, particularly if the invasion of the Japanese home islands occurred. Hence, U.S. miliary strategists were eager to have Soviet participation in order to bring the Pacific war to an early close. The Soviet Union had remained essentially neutral throughout the entire conflict in the Pacific, devoting her resources primarily to the European theater. Thus, in 1944, a serious effort was made to discover how and on what terms the USSR could be brought into the war against Japan.

As part of its vision of the post-war world, the United States anticipated the emergence of a strong China, united under Nationalist control and recognized by both the USSR and Great Britain as an equal in international deliberations. Above all, the United States looked forward to a China friendly to the West and particularly to the United States itself. However, in planning the military campaign in the Pacific, the United States did not fully visualize the political implications of Japan's unconditional surrender. It was assumed, at least by some American leaders, that the Allied Powers, in their efforts to create a free, new world, would not be swayed by matters of selfish national interest.

During the war no carefully conceived plans had been made with respect to the future of the Chinese borderlands. For the most part it was agreed that Chinese sovereignty should be established over those territories which had been taken by Japan. But of the traditional ambitions of others in the Far East, above all, those of China's giant neighbor, the Soviet Union, there was little understanding. The Soviet Union would undoubtedly be keenly interested in the details of any settlement with Japan. Hence, after Russia's entry into the Pacific war against Japan, it was necessary for the West to gain some appreciation of the nature of Soviet objectives if post-war stability were to be achieved in the Pacific.

The Declaration of November, 1943, which brought Roosevelt, Churchill, and Chiang Kai-shek together in Cairo, had promised the return to China of all territories taken by Japan—that is, Manchuria, Formosa, and the Pescadores Islands. Although Stalin unofficially approved the Declaration, the Western Allies were dismayed, in the months that followed, to learn of the full extent of Soviet terms as the price for Soviet participation in the war. Clearly the cost to China would be considerable; yet it is likely that the Soviets, like their Allied counterparts, reckoned on a prolonged conflict with Japan.

Without consulting Chiang Kai-shek beforehand, the United States, Great Britain, and the Soviet Union agreed secretly at Yalta,[1] in February, 1945, on the means and conditions whereby the USSR would enter the war. The terms of the agreement dealt particularly with the Manchurian and Mongolian borderlands. The Yalta Agreement, as far as the Soviet Union was concerned, in effect reversed the decision of the Russo-Japanese War. The Soviets were granted a lease on Port Arthur as a naval base and recognition of their pre-eminent position in the commercial port of Dairen, which was to be internationalized. The Chinese Changchun

---

[1] See Herbert Feis, *The China Tangle,* New York: Atheneum, 1965, pp. 240–321.

Railway, that is, the combined Chinese Eastern and South Manchurian Railways, was to be operated by a joint Soviet-Chinese Company. Further, Southern Sakhalin was to be restored to the Soviet Union and, *in addition,* the Soviets were to be accorded the Japanese Kurile Islands, which had never been Russian before, to protect Soviet outlets to the Pacific. As for Outer Mongolia, or the Mongolian People's Republic, the status quo was to be preserved. From the point of view of the Chinese Nationalists, that meant that Outer Mongolia would remain legally an integral part of China. The Yalta Agreement with respect to Chinese territory would require, of course, the concurrence of the Generalissimo and depend on a Sino-Soviet treaty, which the Western Allies would help to bring about.

Because the U.S. believed that the war against Japan could not be readily won, the rapidity and completeness of the Japanese collapse came as a surprise. No one in informed circles in the U.S. had foreseen the ultimate impact of the atomic bomb. Hiroshima was attacked on August 6, 1945, the Soviets entered the war on August 8, quickly sweeping into Manchuria, and, on August 14, the Japanese emperor called for peace. Undoubtedly, the speed with which the war was brought to a successful conclusion surprised the Red Army as well as the Western forces.

It was under these circumstances that the Sino-Soviet Treaty of Friendship and Alliance was signed on the same day Japan surrendered. Under the terms of the treaty, the USSR pledged to recognize and support the Nationalist government and to respect China's sovereignty over Manchuria and Sinkiang. Port Arthur was to serve as a joint naval base and Dairen to function as a free port under Chinese civil administration. The treaty, by implication, was aimed at Japan, the presumed common enemy in the Far East. Chiang Kai-shek, in return for Soviet guarantees, pledged recognition of the independence of the Mongolian People's Republic if the Mongols themselves expressed such a desire in a plebiscite, which would be held at a later date.

It seems likely that the Soviet leaders assumed that a Nationalist government would rule post-war China. There is no evidence to suggest that the Soviets anticipated that a Communist revolution would succeed within the foreseeable future. It is difficult to get a clear impression, therefore, of what the Soviet regime intended to do in Manchuria and Sinkiang—despite the guarantee of Chinese sovereignty. At least, Moscow seemed determined that its influence would be paramount. At any rate, the coming to power of the Chinese Communists in 1949 radically altered the entire Far Eastern situation. It led, among other things, to the imposition of firm Peking control in the strategic Chinese borderlands to the exclusion of the Soviet Union.

In 1927 Chiang Kai-shek, who in the early years of his government had the support of the Chinese Communists (as well as of the Soviet Union), turned on the Communists and drove them into the hills of south-central China. Their numbers depleted, their hope of capturing the urban masses gone, the Chinese Communists were compelled to work out their own tactics in the countryside. As we now know, the revolution came to be based on the peasants and not on the proletariat in the strict Marxist tradition. Steadily mounting Nationalist pressure by 1935 forced the Communists to undertake their historic "Long March" into northern Shensi, where they established a new base. There, Mao Tse-tung rose to undisputed leadership of the party.

It was the Japanese invasion of China that ultimately made possible the emergence of the Communists as a major factor in Chinese politics. The war led to the formation of a United Front, an uneasy truce which, from 1937 on, enabled Mao to implement his policy of "70 per cent self-development, 20 per cent compromise, and 10 per cent fighting the Japanese." Meanwhile, as the struggle with Japan developed into World War II, China was steadily devastated and the people became increasingly war-weary. When the conflict ended in 1945, the country was prostrate, but the people were reportedly optimistic about the future. The situation offered promising opportunities to the Communists, particularly when the Nationalists seemed unable to cope with the intricate problems of restoring order to the formerly occupied and war-ravaged areas of the country. Attempts on the part of the United States to bring some kind of unity to China through the formation of a coalition government failed. The civil war that had been latent since 1927 and had occasionally erupted in hostilities broke out afresh and swept over the northern provinces of the country.

Though no one could envisage what the "brave new world" would be like once the World War had come to an end, there were expectations that in the settlement would be a plan to resolve, efficiently and amicably, disputes among nations as they arose. There were those, too, who from their study of history were not inclined to look for any radical departure in the conduct of world affairs. Such a person was George Kennan, long a careful student and analyst of the Soviet Union, and in 1945 U.S. *chargé d'affaires* in Moscow. In a telegram to Averell Harriman in Washington on April 23, 1945, he indicated what he anticipated post-war Soviet policy in Asia would be.[2]

I am persuaded [he said] that the future Soviet policy respecting China will continue what it has been in the past: a fluid resilient policy directed at the achievement of maximum power with minimum responsibility . . . the exertion of pressure in various areas in direct proportion to their strategic importance and their proximity to the Soviet frontier . . . domination of the provinces of China in Central Asia contiguous to the Soviet frontier.

The Soviet intervention in the Chinese borderlands during the period 1945-49 clearly demonstrated the insight that Kennan revealed in his telegram.

2 Allen S. Whiting and General Sheng Shih-ts'ai, *Sinkiang: Pawn or Pivot?* East Lansing: Michigan State University Press, 1958, p. 108.

MANCHURIA

The Red Army encountered little opposition from the Japanese in its sweep over Manchuria in mid-August, 1945. After a minimum of fighting, the Japanese forces surrendered. Red Army troops took over the railways, the industries, and the ports; widespread looting occurred and whatever could be transported back to the Soviet Union was confiscated. In this way, the Soviets systematically stripped the Manchurian industrial base of all its essentials. The cost of restoring the industry, which, because it was located in the south, had not been damaged during the Japanese war (although it was later further wrecked during the Civil War), was subsequently estimated at 2 billion U.S. dollars. This ruthless destruction of the Manchurian "Ruhr," as western historians have since pointed out, raises the question whether the Soviets expected an early victory of the Chinese Communists. At any rate, the Red Army violated the Yalta Agreement by remaining in Manchuria after the hostilities with Japan had ended. When they did withdraw in April, 1946, they did so only after they had completed their rape of the productive province and Manchuria had been thoroughly infiltrated by Chinese Communists units armed largely with confiscated Japanese weapons. The Nationalist armies moved into the cities of Manchuria, but the Communists spread throughout the countryside. Unquestionably, the presence of Soviet troops facilitated the spread of Communist power in Manchuria, especially in the north and center. In its dealings with the Nationalists, the Soviet government attempted, for the most part, to be correct: yet it did nothing to assist the Nationalists in reestablishing an administration in a Manchuria that the Red Army had crippled. What is not so clear throughout these months, however, is the nature of the relations between the Soviet and Chinese Communist Parties.

Throughout 1946, nevertheless, Chiang was able to control the situation. But the balance began tipping in 1947–48 in favor of the Communists. By the end of 1948, the Communists had occupied

Mukden, the last Nationalist stronghold in southern Manchuria, and the civil war then moved south of the Great Wall. Early in 1949 Peking fell and, by the summer, Shanghai. On October 1, the establishment of a new Communist government was announced; it was promptly recognized the next day by the USSR. By the end of the year, all mainland China had come under Communist rule, and the Nationalists were established on their island stronghold, Taiwan (Formosa). Early in 1950, after a visit by Mao to Moscow, China and Russia abrogated their old treaties and entered into new agreements.

MONGOLIA

At Yalta, in early 1945, it will be recalled, Stalin had secured an agreement from the United States and Great Britain that the MPR would become independent of China in law as well as in fact. The Sino-Soviet Treaty later that year pledged China to recognize the independence of Mongolia in her existing borders, to be confirmed later by a plebiscite in that republic. The plebiscite was held on October 20, 1945, supervised by the Soviets, and the Mongolians voted almost 100 percent for independence. In January, 1946, Nationalist China recognized the independence of the MPR. Thus, a quarter of a century after the "war of liberation," the legal separation of Outer Mongolia from China, under whose tutelage it had been since the end of the 17th century, was formally effected. But this independence, in reality, had little meaning for the Mongols themselves, who since the early 1920's had been under Soviet domination.[3] While maintaining a hold on Outer Mongolia, Moscow also gave evidence of its intention to interfere in the affairs of Inner Mongolia, with the ultimate objective of linking Inner Mongolia to the MPR.[4]

[3] George G. S. Murphy, *Soviet Mongolia: A Study of the Oldest Political Satellite,* Berkeley and Los Angeles: University of California Press, 1966, 224 pp.

[4] Klaus Mehnert, *Peking and Moscow,* New York: G. P. Putnam's Sons, 1963, p. 263.

In 1947 the Mongol republic adopted a five-year plan of the Soviet type and in 1949 amended its 1940 constitution to make it more like its Soviet model. Russian cultural influence also became dominant, especially after the Cyrillic alphabet was officially introduced to replace the traditional Mongol script. Finally in 1949 the Soviet regime undertook to construct a railway south from the Trans-Siberian to Ulan Bator.

In the immediate post-war years, therefore, Soviet control of the life of the republic intensified. It was in part because of this development that Chiang Kai-shek reversed his support for the admission of Mongolia to the United Nations and in 1947 (and thereafter until 1961) vetoed it.[5]

SINKIANG

Under the terms of the Sino-Soviet Treaty of August, 1945, the USSR promised to respect China's sovereignty in Sinkiang. Stalin asserted that he had no territorial claims on China. Yet clearly the Soviet Union was interested in Sinkiang—and particularly in the Eastern Turkestan Republic, which included that portion of the province containing the richest mineral resources.

In the agreement that was finally signed with the native rebel forces in Urumchi in June, 1946, major concessions to regional autonomy were granted by Chang. In effect, this meant a tacit recognition of a Soviet sphere in Sinkiang. The concessions, as Allen Whiting pointed out in his book *Sinkiang: Pawn or Pivot?*, represented a search "for a compromise solution which might restrain Soviet backing of the rival Chinese Communists" elsewhere in China.[6] But in the months that followed, conflicts developed within

---

[5] Owen Lattimore maintains that Chiang withdrew his approval of Mongolian membership because of the frontier difficulties between Mongolia and Nationalist China, and not because of any Chinese claim to sovereignty over Mongolia as Western newspapers at the time stated. See his "Communism, Mongolian Brand," *The Atlantic Monthly*, Sept., 1962, p. 80. However, whatever Nationalist claim there is to Outer Mongolia now dates from 1953, when the Sino-Soviet treaty of 1945 was nullified.

[6] *Ibid.*, p. 110.

the rebel republic, and ultimately the name of the republic was dropped.

In the meantime Uighur Nationalists in the Tarim Basin took advantage of Chinese preoccupation with the Kuldja rebellion to demand an independent Turkestani state. The leaders of the movement envisaged an authoritarian state, embracing not only the Turks of Sinkiang, but also their cousins in Soviet Central Asia, including in their dream even the Yakuts of northeastern Siberia. Though anti-Communist as well as anti-Russian in outlook, the Pan-Turkists established friendly relations with the rebels in Kuldja. The Kuomintang was unable to deal with this new threat; above all, Chiang did not oppose the movement, probably because he feared that he might push the Uighurs into close association with leftist elements. At any rate, the Chinese Nationalists came to terms with the Uighurs and in May, 1947 appointed a Uighur to head the regional government. However, this act did not provide a solution, for the governor was more Uighur than Kuomintang. Indeed, the governor went so far as to seek outside support for his ideas by establishing relations with the United States mission in Urumchi. Finally, in December, 1948, Chiang removed the governor, but the internal political situation in China proper had so changed that little if any action could be taken in Sinkiang.

There were additional troubles for the Kuomintang in Sinkiang. In September, 1946, Soviet and Mongol troops invaded the Altay district of Sinkiang, creating the so-called Pietashan Affair. The invading forces justified their attack by claiming that the area was rightfully a part of Outer Mongolia and had been so as late as 1919. Because the Mongols of the Altay had not fought alongside the Outer Mongols in 1911 to oust the Chinese from the plateau, the Chinese Republican government had detached the Altay district from Mongolia and added it to Sinkiang. The Russians denied their participation in the affair, but the Chinese Nationalists denounced Soviet strategy and denied Outer Mongolian claims.

Although the Nationalists refused to enter into any new agreements with the Soviets for joint economic development of Sinkiang, they did, in May, 1949, surrender virtual control over the air route between Alma-Ata and Hami, via Urumchi. Such was Soviet policy that while the Chinese Communists were rapidly advancing throughout China proper, the Russians still found it wise to seek or force concessions from the Nationalists in Sinkiang.

Finally, on September 26, 1949, as Chinese Communist units were approaching from the east, the Chinese governor of Sinkiang declared the province a part of Communist China. On October 13, the troops entered Sinkiang. The armed local rebel forces were disbanded, and their leaders purged. Others despaired of their position. When the Communists took Urumchi, some 3,000 Kazakhs began to move out. Fleeing southward, they passed through the Tien-Shan and skirted Lob Nor, before heading into the rugged Altyn Tagh. But of the 3,000 herdsmen who left Sinkiang, only a small remnant reached India late in 1951 after a horrifying experience en route.

1950 TO THE OUTBREAK OF THE CONTROVERSY

The establishment of a Chinese Communist regime in Peking seemed to many Western observers to mark the beginning of a new era in Asia, one which would have far-reaching implications for the entire world. It seemed to portend, above all, the emergence of a new set of political-geographical relationships, based to a very important degree on ideological unity between the two Communist powers, the Soviet Union and the People's Republic of China. These new relationships were to have, in the decade following 1950, a significant bearing on the development of the Chinese border territories.

Hitherto, Russian expansion in East and Inner Asia, whether of the Tsarist or Soviet variety, had occurred mainly at the expense of a weak and disorganized China. Indeed, the very weakness of China had encouraged and facilitated Russian expansion, no less than it had stimulated the imperial rivalry there of Japan, Germany, France, and Great Britain. The Communist success, however, brought to an end foreign overseas intervention in Chinese affairs. Equally significant, it compelled the Soviets to reassess their policy toward the Chinese state. Thereafter, Soviet strategy in Asia would have to contend with the fact of effective Chinese control in the borderlands. But this control would now be imposed by the Communist Party of China, ideologically linked to the Communist Party of the Soviet Union. Hence, Chinese Communist ascendancy would bring to an end the role traditionally played by Manchuria and Sinkiang as pawns in Asia. It would lead, too, to the emergence of a recognized Chinese interest in Outer Mongolia, where for nearly thirty years the influence of the Soviet Union had been paramount.

Immediately following the revolution, the new Chinese regime took a number of steps to organize both Sinkiang and Manchuria and to integrate them into the body politic of China. Soviet official influence and control, which had survived or re-emerged there after World War II, were, by a series of agreements, gradually reduced and finally liquidated. Although Soviet and Chinese Communist maps and atlases revealed discrepancies in the Pamirs and at the confluence of the Amur and Ussuri Rivers, these did not appear to be of enough importance at the time to disturb the ideological unity of the two powers or the stability of either the Inner Asian or the Far Eastern borderlands. News dispatches out of Formosa and India from time to time mentioned opposition of the native Turks to the Communists in Sinkiang, but other reports suggested convincingly that the Chinese were capable of handling any disorder that developed there. Hence, for the first time in decades—and indeed, one might argue, in history—Sinkiang and Manchuria had become truly oriented toward Peking.

In the Mongolian People's Republic, on the other hand, the Soviet Union was able after 1950 to preserve its hegemony. The Chinese Communists, however, were quick to follow their recognition of Mongolian independence with the establishment of an impressive and sizable embassy in Ulan Bator. Indeed, there were some who remembered that as far back as 1936 Mao Tse-tung, the future Communist leader of China, had said in a talk with the American writer, Edgar Snow, that with the victory of the people's revolution in China, the MPR would "automatically become" a part of China.[7] At any rate, cultural exchange and economic aid agreements between Peking and Ulan Bator in 1952 and 1955 resulted in a large influx of Chinese workers into Mongolia to assist in major construction projects. Chinese interest in Mongolia was evident; but the Mongols were aware of it and the Soviets were apparently willing to give aid and economic development jointly with the Chinese. What Moscow might do if its pre-eminent role in Mongolia were challenged or if the political status of Mongolia were openly questioned by Peking, was at that time a matter only for speculation among Western authorities. Within Mongolia, the presence of large numbers of Chinese (workers and their families) did not seem to create any problem for the Mongols, in spite of traditional antipathy. It was impossible, however, to determine the true feelings of the Mongols, who remained effectively isolated from the outside world. At any rate, the Mongols stood to benefit from both the USSR and the CPR, so long as unity and friendship prevailed. Undoubtedly, it was the profession of unity which served to minimize the importance of Mongolian-Chinese boundary discrepancies. The skirmishes that had occurred, for example, between the Chinese Nationalists and the Mongols in the Altay region ended when the Communists took over Sinkiang.

In recognizing officially the independence of the MPR, the Chinese Communists also gave tacit approval to the Soviet annexation of the Mongol region of Urianghay, or Tannu-Tuva. At the time of formal incorporation of the territory into the USSR in 1944, Tannu-Tuva possessed some strategic value for the Russians. Under Russian control, it afforded a shorter and generally more favorable border with the MPR or with Nationalist China (should

[7] Reported in *Mongolia Today,* Sept.–Oct., 1964, p. 4.

FIGURE 1

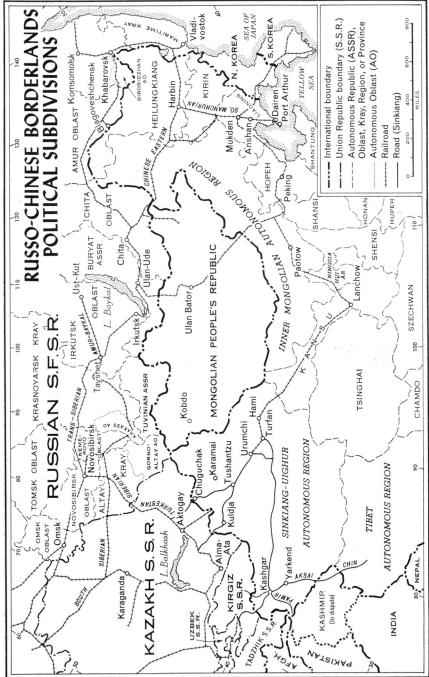

RUSSO-CHINESE BORDERLANDS
POLITICAL SUBDIVISIONS

International boundary (S.S.R.)
Union Republic boundary (S.S.R.)
Autonomous Republic (ASSR),
Oblast, Kray, Region, or Province
Autonomous Oblast (AO)
Railroad
Road (Sinkiang)

MILES
0   200   400   600   800

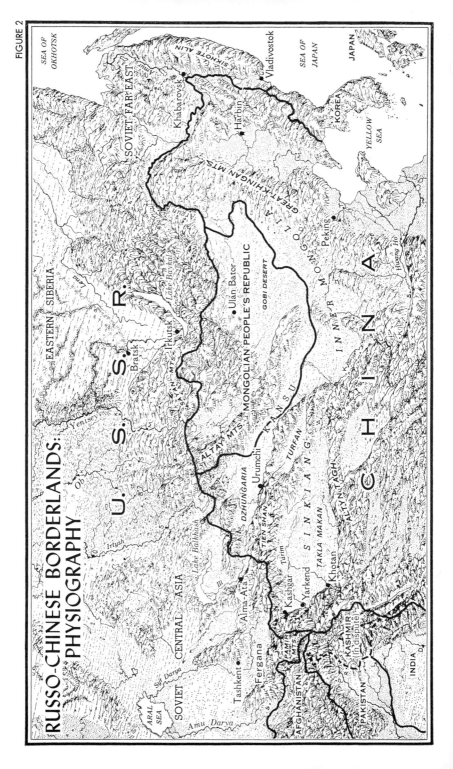

FIGURE 2

RUSSO-CHINESE BORDERLANDS: PHYSIOGRAPHY

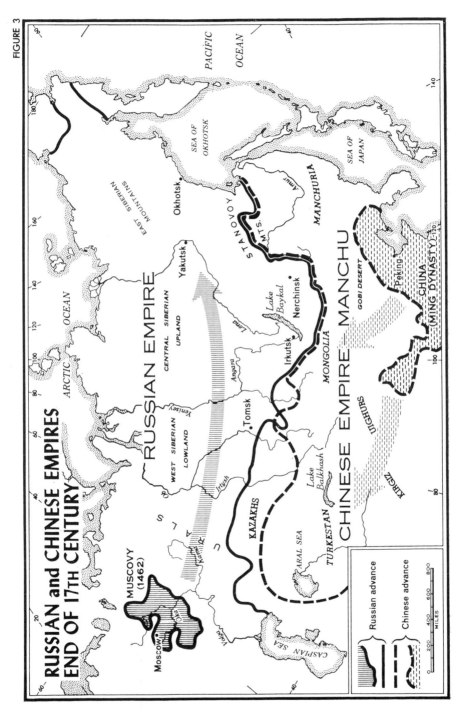

FIGURE 3

RUSSIAN and CHINESE EMPIRES
END OF 17TH CENTURY

DISTRIBUTION OF MAIN ETHNIC GROUPS IN THE RUSSO-CHINESE BORDERLANDS

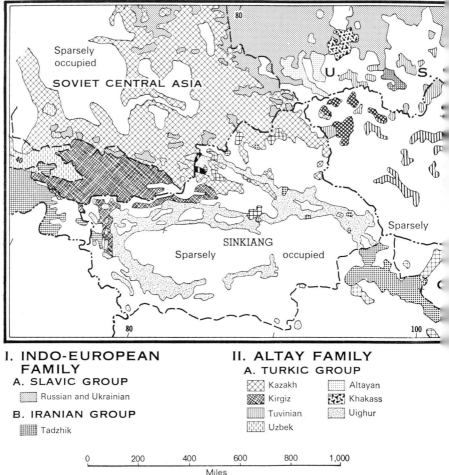

I. INDO-EUROPEAN FAMILY

A. SLAVIC GROUP

Russian and Ukrainian

B. IRANIAN GROUP

Tadzhik

II. ALTAY FAMILY

A. TURKIC GROUP

Kazakh

Kirgiz

Tuvinian

Uzbek

Altayan

Khakass

Uighur

0   200   400   600   800   1,000

Miles

FIGURE 4

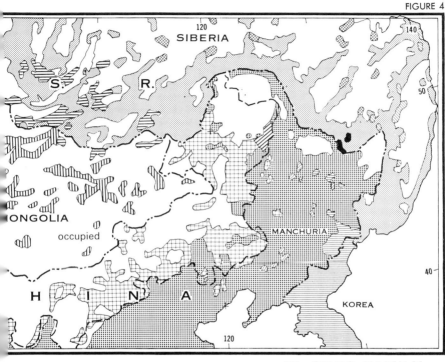

B. TUNGUS-MANCHURIAN GROUP

▨ Evenki	▨ Manchu	
▨ Nenets and related groups	■ Sibo	
	▤ Korean	

C. MONGOL GROUP

▤ Buryat	▨ Daurian	
▥ Khalkha	▨ Other Mongol groups	
▦ Mongol (Inner Mongol)		

III. SINIC FAMILY

▦ Han and Dungan

IV. SEMITIC FAMILY

■ Jewish

—·—·— International boundary

— — — Internal boundary

FIGURE 5

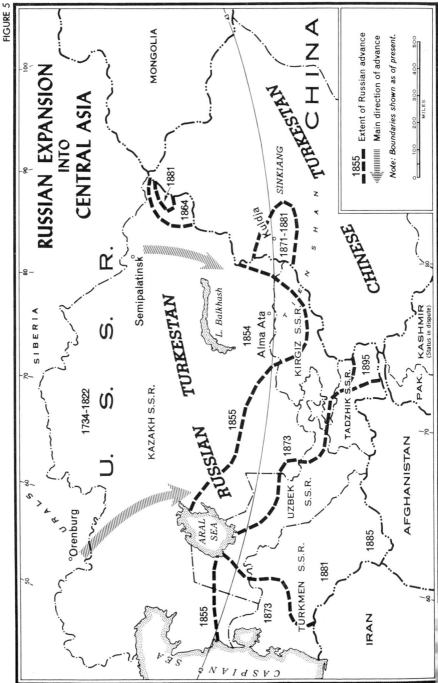

RUSSIAN EXPANSION INTO CENTRAL ASIA

1855 — Extent of Russian advance
Main direction of advance
Note: *Boundaries shown as of present.*

FIGURE 6

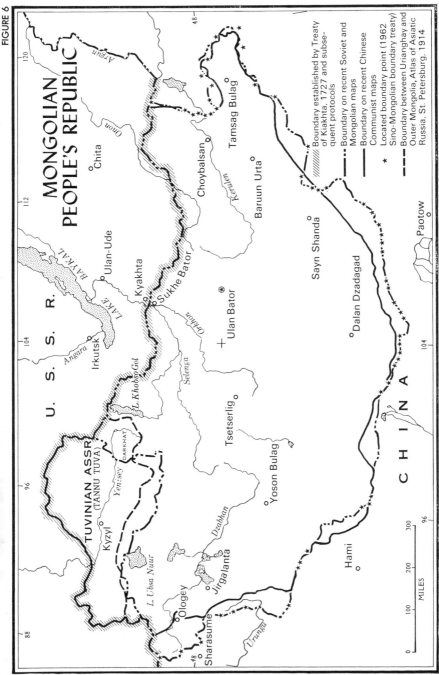

MONGOLIAN
PEOPLE'S REPUBLIC

U. S. S. R.

Chita

LAKE BAYKAL

Ulan-Ude

Irkutsk

Angara

Kyakhta

Sukhe Bator

L. Khobso Gol

Ulan Bator

Orkhon

Selenga

TUVINIAN ASSR
(TANNU TUVA)

DARKHAT

Kyzyl

Yenisey

Tsetserlig

L. Ubsa Nuur

Dzabhan

Ologey

Jirgalanta

Sharasume

Urungu

Yoson Bulag

Hami

CHINA

Sayn Shanda

Dalan Dzadagad

Baruun Urta

Kerulen

Tamsag Bulag

Choybalsan

Onon

Argun

Paotow

Boundary established by Treaty
of Kiakhta, 1727 and subsequent protocols

Boundary on recent Soviet and
Mongolian maps

Boundary on recent Chinese
Communist maps

★   Located boundary point (1962
Sino-Mongolian boundary treaty)

Boundary between Urianghay and
Outer Mongolia, Atlas of Asiatic
Russia, St. Petersburg, 1914

MILES

0   100   200   300

FIGURE 7

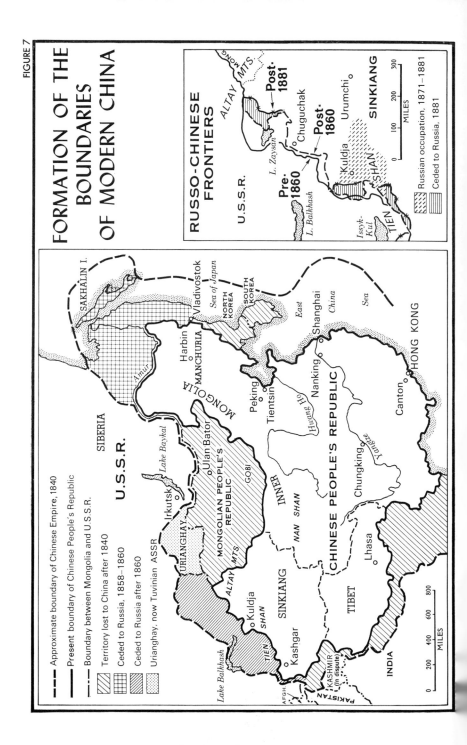

FORMATION OF THE BOUNDARIES OF MODERN CHINA

RUSSO-CHINESE FRONTIERS

U.S.S.R.

ALTAY MTS.

SNOWG MONG

Post- 1881

L. Zaysan

Pre- 1860

Chuguchak

Post- 1860

L. Balkhash

Kuldja

Chuguchak

Urumchi

SINKIANG

TIEN SHAN

Issyk-Kul

MILES
0   100   200   300

Russian occupation, 1871–1881

Ceded to Russia, 1881

SAKHALIN I.

SIBERIA

U.S.S.R.

Amur

MANCHURIA

Harbin

Vladivostok

Sea of Japan

NORTH KOREA

SOUTH KOREA

Peking

Tientsin

East

China

Sea

Shanghai

Nanking

Huang Ho

Lake Baykal

Irkutsk

Ulan Bator

MONGOLIA

MONGOLIAN PEOPLE'S REPUBLIC

URIANGHAY

GOBI

INNER

NAN SHAN

ALTAY MTS.

CHINESE PEOPLE'S REPUBLIC

Chungking

Yangtze

Canton

HONG KONG

SINKIANG

TIEN SHAN

Kuldja

Kashgar

Lhasa

TIBET

INDIA

KASHMIR (In dispute)

PAKISTAN

AFGH.

Lake Balkhash

- ─ ─ ─ Approximate boundary of Chinese Empire, 1840
- ───── Present boundary of Chinese People's Republic
- ─ · ─ · Boundary between Mongolia and U.S.S.R.

Territory lost to China after 1840

Ceded to Russia, 1858–1860

Ceded to Russia after 1860

Urianghay, now Tuvinian ASSR

MILES
0   200   400   600   800

the latter have succeeded in gaining full possession of Outer Mongolia). Moreover, the upland region, bounded on the north by the Sayan Mountains and on the south by the Tannu-Ola Range, lies astride the most direct route between western Siberia and the western Mongolian centers of Kobdo and Uliassutay. But perhaps of even more value to the Russians is the mineral wealth of the region. Not only is Tannu-Tuva, or the Tuvinian ASSR, rich in coal, but it also has important deposits of asbestos, salt, gold, and copper.

Development of these resources, however, continues to remain in the first stages. While a good motor road connects the capital, Kyzyl, with Abakan to the north of the Sayan, the region still has, as far as is known, no direct rail link with the rest of the Soviet Union.

Of the more than 200,000 inhabitants of the autonomous republic, at least half are Russians, the bulk of whom live in the capital and in other populated points. Though the countryside may remain Tuvinian, for all purposes Tannu-Tuva has become irrevocably Russian.

It should be emphasized that the Chinese Communists were, and still are, dedicated to world revolution and internationalism. These objectives they shared with their Soviet counterparts, who remained until the latter half of the 1950's under the influence of Stalinism. All other interests for the most part played, or seemed to play, a subordinate role. To promote international communism (and Sino-Soviet interests), the leaders of both countries pledged themselves to friendship. The advantages that would ensue from ideological unity would outweigh any legacy of the past that might disrupt the association. Sino-Soviet friendship, however, was not a partnership between equals. Rather, it represented the adherence of the Chinese Communists to the bloc led by the USSR. Ideological unity enhanced the strength of the bloc, if measured only in terms of legions; at the same time it made possible Soviet aid to China in its vast program of reconstruction.

WITHDRAWAL OF THE SOVIETS FROM
MANCHURIA AND SINKIANG

Shortly after the formation of the new government in Peking in September–October, 1949, Mao Tse-tung left for Moscow on his first visit to the USSR. His negotiations there with Premier Stalin, culminating in February, 1950, in a Treaty of Friendship, Alliance and Mutual Aid, laid the basis for a new Sino-Soviet state relationship. The agreements held a special significance for Manchuria and Sinkiang.

Although the Soviets did not agree to an immediate departure from Manchuria, they did make concessions. Until a peace treaty was signed with Japan, but not later than the end of 1952, the Soviets intended to remain on in Manchuria. They agreed to share administration with the Chinese of the Changchun Railway. They assumed the role of garrisoning Port Arthur, but the base would be used jointly with the Chinese. Dairen, the main port of the southern terminus of the Manchurian railway system, was transferred to Chinese civil administration. Several joint-stock enterprises were also agreed on, including a shipbuilding and repair company at Dairen.

With respect to Sinkiang, the Soviets and the Chinese agreed in March, 1950, on the establishment of similar joint-stock companies to exploit oil and nonferrous metals. The capital, control, and profits were to be shared for 30 years. Some Western observers claimed that these joint-stock enterprises represented a continuation of Soviet interest in Sinkiang's resources. Undoubtedly this was true; yet at the same time, in the early years of the Chinese Communist takeover in Sinkiang, the Chinese needed whatever assistance the Soviets could or would give, especially since the latter in past decades had already been active there. At any rate, it was clear that the Chinese intended to make Sinkiang Chinese, for in March Peking announced a program for large-scale immigration into the northwestern province.

Finally, the agreements reached in Moscow pertained also to the organization and operation of civilian airlines between Peking and Chita, Peking and Irkutsk, and Peking and Alma-Ata.

In 1952, since no peace treaty with Japan was forthcoming, the Soviets complied with the terms of the 1950 treaty and transferred, without compensation, the Changchun Railway to Chinese administration. Soviet forces, however, remained in Port Arthur, largely because of the Korean War and, reportedly, at China's suggestion and request. Two years later, following the visit of Khrushchev and Bulganin to Peking, the Soviets agreed to transfer their shares in the Manchurian joint-stock companies to China, and in 1955 they withdrew their garrison from Port Arthur. Thus, ten years after they had entered Manchuria to fight the Japanese and five years after the Chinese Communist victory over the Nationalists there, Soviet forces were withdrawn to Russian territory. Apart from the fact that Soviet engineers and other technical personnel remained to assist in the reconstruction of Manchuria, the Soviets acknowledged Chinese supremacy in Manchuria.

During the Khrushchev mission to China, it was agreed that the Soviets would transfer to China their shares in the Sinkiang joint mining companies. These companies had not accomplished very much beyond planning activities and training Chinese and native Sinkiang personnel. The greatest progress had been made in the oil industry, including considerable drilling and the construction of an automatic cracking plant equipped with Soviet machinery. The transfer of shares began in 1955, and the companies were reorganized as Chinese state-owned enterprises. Finally, as a result of an agreement in October, 1954, the Soviets and Chinese planned to link the Turk-Sib Railway with the Lanchow-Sinkiang Railway, which the Chinese had begun building in 1952. Thus, as in Manchuria, the Soviets by 1955 had surrendered their "sphere of influence" and had allowed the Chinese to take over full control and direction of Sinkiang's economic development.

CHINESE COMMUNIST REORGANIZATION OF THE BORDERLANDS

Political Reorganization. Like the USSR, the CPR is a land of different national or ethnic groups. The diversity in China, however, is considerably less than that in the Soviet Union. The Han-Chinese, like their Slavic or Russian counterparts to the north, predominate. But whereas the Slavs constitute three-fourths of the USSR's population, and the Russians alone slightly less, the Han-Chinese account for 94 percent of China's population.

The national minorities of China inhabit primarily the border areas, that is, those around the periphery of China proper. The border territories, especially on the north and east, as we have seen, are large and strategic and, in the drier areas, sparsely settled. Although rich in resources, these territories had remained, with the exception of Manchuria, undeveloped. Whatever material progress there had been had been prompted, certainly until the end of World War II, by Russians or Japanese, not by the native peoples themselves nor by the Chinese. It should be kept in mind, too, that the national groups of the borderlands are related to similar ethnic and culture groups in the Soviet Union. Moreover, to add another complicating factor, some of these peoples, notably the Muslim Uighurs of Sinkiang, are traditionally anti-Chinese, and even the semi-nomadic Inner Mongols had cause to resent the encroachment of the Chinese farmer on their ancient grazing lands.

As they were consolidating their hold on the mainland, the Chinese Communists were compelled to make concessions to the minority groups in an attempt to allay their fears and suspicions. When they had secured effective control, however, they introduced a policy, based on that evolved in the Soviet Union, designed to eliminate national aspirations and in effect to destroy the bases of the native cultures.

The nationalities policy required the setting up of a hierarchy of national territorial units to represent fixed and stable ethnic groups in an attempt to create the illusion of local or regional autonomy. Within such territories, native culture forms were permitted to survive, even though the social fabric was to be remodeled along lines determined by the party leaders. The net result of such a policy, if carried to the ultimate, would mean the death of any true national identity and of the traditions of a proud people inherited from time immemorial. Whatever promotes "friendship" and "unity" between the minorities and the predominant group was to be permitted and encouraged; whatever revealed basic historic antagonisms between the peoples and stimulated the desire for separation and national independence would be suppressed and destroyed. Moreover, the party leaders were not above rewriting history to "verify" their point of view should it be necessary.

Constitutionally, the Soviet Union is a union of the federative type, consisting at present of 15 republics. These were established for compact national groups that totaled a million or more and lived along the borders of the country. The fact of their location is important, according to the Soviet constitution, because it permits the people to secede. This right, however, is purely a theoretical one; to date, no republics have seceded, nor is the desire for secession ever allowed to express itself. Prior to their victory in 1949, the Chinese Communists may have entertained the idea of a federal structure for China, but the republic was organized as a unitary state. Because of the overwhelming size of the Han-Chinese majority, the Chinese Communists may conceivably have felt that the minority groups were not important enough numerically to warrant supporting the myth of a federation of free and equal peoples. At any rate, within the unitary state framework, the Chinese established a hierarchy of national regions, but it was considerably less elaborate than that in existence in the Soviet Union.

At the highest level of the structure were the autonomous regions, or ch'u, which may be compared to the Union republics, except for the fact that the regions were not given the right to secede. Next in the hierarchy were the autonomous districts, or chow, and below the chow, the autonomous areas, or hsien, and banners, or ch'i. The political-administrative delineation of China which persists to the present came about mainly after 1953.

In Manchuria, between August, 1949, and November, 1952, there existed what in effect amounted to an autonomous Communist regime. The Northeast People's Government had been established, because Manchuria was the most advanced territory from the point of view of Communist power consolidation. The country was then divided into five provinces and a national region. Subsequently, in November, 1952, after the Northeast Government had been abolished, Manchuria was reorganized. In June, 1954, a second reorganization followed, but Manchuria was not accorded national autonomy. Obviously, the complete Sinification of the Manchu peoples there (today numbering over two and a half million) as a result of the considerable Chinese migration was an important element working against autonomy. But the overriding industrial importance to China of Manchuria, along with other political considerations, was more telling. Consequently, the Chinese Communists rejected the term "Manchuria" and referred henceforth to the region as Tungpei, or the Northeast.

The drier western part, the Khingan region, was detached from historic Manchuria and, with its Mongol population, transferred to an enlarged Inner Mongolia. The Northeast, therefore, includes three provinces: Heilungkiang, Kirin, and Liaoning. Heilungkiang, the largest province, faces the Soviet Far East across the Amur and Ussuri Rivers. The province of Kirin to the south borders in part on the Korean People's Republic. South of Kirin is Liaoning, which includes the industrial core of old Manchuria. The Northeast encompasses some 300,000 square miles and contains close to 50 million inhabitants, mainly Chinese. Several autonomous areas were established for the scattered groups of Mongols that remained, while some half-million culturally-tenacious Koreans, along the eastern border of Kirin, formed the Yen-Pien Autonomous District.

As early as 1947, the Chinese Communists proclaimed an Inner

Mongolian Autonomous Region—and thus outmaneuvered the Soviets. In the decade following, the boundaries of the region were considerably enlarged. Of all the minority groups, the Inner Mongols have undoubtedly been courted the most, and for a variety of interesting political reasons. When the Japanese occupied parts of Inner Mongolia, they made a conscious effort to win the favor of the native peoples—and not without some success. The Russians, too, because of their role in the MPR had good reason to be interested in the future of Inner Mongolia. The proclamation by the Chinese Communists, in the immediate post-war period, of the Inner Mongolian Autonomous Region unquestionably won the Inner Mongols to the side of the revolution. Yet in the new, enlarged Inner Mongolia the Mongols were outnumbered by Chinese by at least five to one; in the southeast, where most of the Chinese agriculturalists were settled, the ratio was probably even higher. Nevertheless, there are more Mongols in the CPR than in the MPR or in the USSR, and they are identified through the autonomous region. The construction in 1953 of a tomb for Genghis Khan in Inner Mongolia also seemed to be a part of the overall appeal to the Mongols, for among all Mongols the story of the great warrior-leader has remained very much alive.

Sinkiang to the west of Inner Mongolia, beyond Kansu, is ethnically more complex. When Chinese Communist control had finally been effected there, perhaps sometime in 1955, the Sinkiang-Uighur Autonomous Region was created in recognition of the predominant ethnic group, the Uighurs.

However, like the Soviets, the Chinese Communists rejected the Pan-Turkic argument that all the Turkic-speaking peoples of both Soviet Central Asia and Sinkiang belong to one single nation. Rather, the position adopted in the CPR, as in the USSR, was that the Turkic peoples constitute several groups. The Chinese Communists stressed the historic differences between the various groups —the Kazakhs, the Uzbeks, the Kirgiz, the Uighurs, and others— ignoring the similarities that prevail, or the feelings of mutual kinship that may exist. Thus, within the Sinkiang-Uighur Autonomous Region were set up subordinate units representing Turkic non-Uighur minorities. There are, in addition, other subordinate units for Mongols, as well as for the Tadzhiks, the Sibos, and the Dungans. Until 1953, the number of Chinese settlers in Sinkiang remained relatively small. But the Chinese Communists encouraged migration, and it was to be expected that before long the Chinese would outnumber the natives. The exploitation of the rich mineral base, land reclamation, improved communications, and industrial development would all work to the disadvantage of the region's traditional cultures.

In 1956, as part of its program of indoctrination, the Peking regime announced that it would adopt the Cyrillic (Russian) alphabet for the Mongolian and Turkic languages of Inner Mongolia and Sinkiang. This would have made it possible for the Uighurs and the Inner Mongols to read materials published in the Soviet Union for the respective ethnic groups there. Perhaps it was believed in Peking that this would, in effect, speed up indoctrination of China's minorities, and conversely enable the Chinese to influence thinking among the Soviet minorities. However, not long after, the plan was dropped and Premier Chou En-lai indicated that the Latin script rather than the Cyrillic would be introduced for all of China's languages. This change was confirmed two years later in 1960, when it was reported [8] that the Sinkiang-Uighur Regional People's Council had given its approval to replacing with Latin the Arabic script traditionally employed in Uighur and Kazakh writing. The change-over was expected to take from three to five years. Without doubt, the Latinization of the languages of China would facilitate communication within the republic, but it would create a barrier for the peoples on either side of the Sino-Mongolian-Soviet boundary. Ease of communication via the Cyrillic alphabet throughout the Sino-Soviet borderlands could have led to indoctri-

[8] *The New York Times,* March 27, 1960.

nation, but it could just as easily have led to the Russification of China's minorities. Yet the Mongols, Uighurs and other minority groups were told that if they wished advancement within the new China such was possible only through the study of Chinese. To encourage this, the Chinese opened new schools throughout the border territories to teach the Chinese language. It was made sufficiently clear to all that Chinese was to be the official language everywhere.

ECONOMIC REORGANIZATION AND DEVELOPMENT

During their occupation of Manchuria (Manchukuo), the Japanese erected an industrial base well in advance of the rest of China. Not only does the region possess large reserves of coal, oil shale, iron ore and other minerals, but its upland forests are valuable, the energy potential of its rivers is considerable, and its agriculture is capable of producing surpluses. The Japanese greatly increased the output of fuels and minerals, built power stations, double-tracked and extended the railways, and erected a complex of manufacturing establishments second in the Far East only to the home industry of Japan itself.

The economic importance of Manchuria to China was fully appreciated by both the Chinese Nationalists and the Communists in 1945. Chiang Kai-shek was determined to establish Nationalist control there, but was frustrated by the Soviets. When he finally lost the struggle with the Communists, the latter won Manchuria but were compelled to accept, without apparent complaint, an industrial machine that had been crippled by the Red Army. Furthermore, as the Japanese workers returned to their homes in Japan, the Chinese were left without the skills to operate the establishments. Thus, the new Communist rulers of Manchuria were confronted with an enormous task, that of rebuilding a shattered economy. But with subsequent material and technical aid from the USSR and some of its East European satellites, the Chinese succeeded in reestablishing the Northeast as China's major industrial center.

In the early years, recovery was reported by the Communists to have been rapid. Up until 1951 the task had involved simply restoration and reconstruction of the former industrial base. In 1951 the Chinese, in addition to undertaking further large-scale restoration and reconstruction, began planning new enterprises. It is doubtful, however, in spite of Communist claims to the contrary, that by 1953 they had restored Manchuria's industry to its pre-1945 level. Published Communist data of the period seem inflated beyond all credence.

From the Communist point of view, the overwhelming industrial concentration in the Northeast was irrational, and in the First Five-Year Plan (1953–57) Peking was determined to create new manufacturing centers elsewhere. In effect this effort achieved mainly an expansion in the Northeast's old plant capacity but little new construction. Since the emphasis was on heavy industry, the Anshan Iron and Steel Works, the heart of the complex, was restored and expanded. Accordingly, by 1958 Anshan produced 4.5 million tons of steel compared to a peak output of half a million tons under the Japanese. Similarly, expansion of the Penki Iron and Steel Works occurred, although a new plant was started at Fushun. Mukden continued to be the major center for the manufacturing of machinery of all types. However, at Harbin in the north, new construction gave that city more weight in the industrial structure of the Northeast than it had previously possessed. At least five enterprises were established there with Soviet aid during the First Five-Year Plan. It thus became a major center for the production of equipment for the electric power industry, which would undoubtedly have contributed to the proposed joint Sino-Soviet development of the water resources of the Amur Basin.

Despite the industrial recovery the Northeast remained essentially agricultural. Even though it had become a land of large cities (Table VII), four-fifths of its population remained on farms. Manchuria's millions of acres of fertile black soil continued to yield large harvests of soybeans, kaoliang, millet, and wheat.

The Japanese evacuation and civil war had a serious effect on Manchuria's agriculture. Recovery, however, was rather rapid. While in 1948 grain production amounted to only 12.8 million tons compared to 18.3 million in 1943, by 1951 it had risen substantially

TABLE VII.

Population of Major Cities of the Northeast (Manchuria)
(1957 estimate)

Anshan, Liaoning	805,000	
Antung, Liaoning	360,000	(1953)
Changchun, Kirin	975,000	
Chinchow, Liaoning	352,000	(1953)
Fushun, Liaoning	985,000	
Harbin, Heilungkiang	1,552,000	
Kirin, Kirin	568,000	
Penki, Liaoning	449,000	(1953)
Tsitsihar, Heilungkiang	668,000	

Source: *Encyclopaedia Britannica World Atlas*, Chicago, 1961, p. 153.

though still falling short of the prewar level. Nevertheless, large quantities of grain were shipped regularly from the Northeast into North China to feed the millions there. In the meantime, a sweeping land reform liquidated landlord holdings which, according to Communist sources, had found 80 percent of the land in the hands of only 10 percent of the rural population.[9]

The collectivization of agriculture began in China after 1951. As the *Human Relations Area Files China Handbook* notes, "the path of collectivization was marked by several distinct stages from mutual-aid teams through agricultural producers' cooperatives to collective farms, and finally to communes."[10] At the same time, large state farms after the Soviet model were set up, particularly in

[9] O. Edmund Clubb, *Chinese Communist Development Programs in Manchuria*, New York: Institute of Pacific Relations, 1954, p. 14.

[10] Hsiao Hsia (ed.), *China: Its People, Its Society, Its Culture*, New Haven: HRAF Press, 1960, p. 340.

areas where reclamation was necessary. This was the case in northern Heilungkiang along the Amur and Sungari Rivers, which attracted new settlers. By 1955, Heilungkiang had 32 mechanized state farms.

The implementation of the Amur Basin development scheme was designed to benefit the industry and agriculture of the entire Sino-Soviet Far Eastern borderlands. The agreement between Moscow and Peking, signed in 1956, called for the construction of a series of hydroelectric installations along the Amur and its tributaries, with a combined capacity of 13 million KW, "sufficient to meet the expected needs of industry, agriculture, and transportation." One Soviet writer referred to the proposed program in terms of a "fourth metallurgical base in the Aldan-Amur region of Eastern Siberia." Others stressed the extent to which such cities as Harbin, Mukden, and even Peking, would benefit from new sources of power. Improvements in the river system, too, would have permitted control of the seasonal flow, eliminated the serious flooding that occurs, and created more favorable conditions for agricultural development on both sides of the river. The agreement, however, was never implemented; with the worsening of Sino-Soviet relations it is doubtful if it ever will be.

In Sinkiang, industrialization also made some progress, but by Western standards it could not be considered impressive. Undoubtedly, distance from China proper, the lack of adequate transportation facilities, and a scarcity of trained or skilled labor remained obvious handicaps.

In the early years of Communist control in Sinkiang considerable use was made of the military. In December, 1949, a decree of the People's Military Revolutionary Council called on the Liberation Army to turn to economic construction. Of the 193,000 soldiers stationed there, reportedly 110,000 were assigned to work in industry and agriculture.

One of the most important tasks to be undertaken was the construction of a railway to link the remote region to central China.

Work was begun on the Lanchow-Sinkiang Railway in 1952. By mid-1960 track had been laid to within 200 miles of Urumchi; but by mid-1961 it remained uncompleted, possibly because of a lack of steel for rails. From Urumchi, it was planned to extend the line westward past the oilfields at Tushantzu, into the Dzhungarian Gate.[11] At the Sino-Soviet border, it was to connect with a Soviet line which the Russians built in 1958 eastward from Aktogay on the Turk-Sib Railway. This vital Eurasian transcontinental line, affording direct rail travel from East Berlin to Hanoi, was to become, however, the first casualty of the Sino-Soviet split. The junction of the Soviet and Chinese lines at the border was never effected.

Other rail lines were planned in Sinkiang, extending northward across Dzhungaria and southward into the Tarim Basin. In mid-1958 surveying began for a Kashgar-Turfan route, which would link both sides of the Tien-Shan. Ultimately, too, Sinkiang was to be joined by rail to Tibet. Simultaneously with the planning of railways, a network of motor highways was developed throughout the region. Strategic roads were extended southward from Kashgar into the Karakorum, and across Outer Ladakh into the Tibetan Autonomous Region. Air transportation over the territory was established on a regular basis also, as a result of the 1950 agreement between Stalin and Mao. And, reportedly, plans were drafted by Kazakh scientists for the construction of a 620-mile waterway linking the Ili, Chu, and Syr-Darya, thus affording Sinkiang a connection by water with the Aral Sea. Another Soviet report also emphasized that northwestern Sinkiang now had an outlet to the Arctic Ocean, due to recent Soviet developments along the Upper Irtysh.

Sinkiang is rich in resources, as was noted in Chapter 1. The largest deposits of oil in China lie within the region, principally at Tushantzu and Karamai. In 1953, with Soviet help, a refinery was constructed at Tushantzu. Karamai was said to be so rich that one

---

[11] A. R. Field, "Strategic Development in Sinkiang," *Foreign Affairs*, January, 1961, p. 315.

well alone produced 30,000 tons of oil in 1959. From Karamai a pipeline was laid to the Tushantzu refinery.

New discoveries of coal raised the estimated reserves to 35 billion tons, of which in 1958 3.6 million tons were mined. There is coal in many places in Sinkiang, particularly near Chuguchak on the Soviet border, at Hami, and near Urumchi. Iron ore, too, is found in large quantities; however, the quality does not seem to be high. At any rate, the poor quality of the ores and poor coking coal slowed the production of steel at the August 1st Iron and Steel Plant (built in 1951) at Urumchi. This handicap in turn, presumably, delayed the laying of track on the Lanchow-Sinkiang Railway.

It was to be expected that the Chinese Communists would give increasing attention to the industrialization of Sinkiang. Not only is industry the key to the transformation of lesser developed minority regions into modern nations, but the Chinese also recognized and affirmed that Sinkiang had all the material prerequisites for becoming a major industrial region of China. In 1959, therefore, the Sinkiang Party Committee adopted a resolution to turn the province into a base for the production of iron and steel, petroleum, coal, nonferrous metals, cotton and other textiles, sugar and other products. And, to overcome the shortage of labor there, workers from the central provinces of China were channelled into the Northwest.

Collectivization brought about a social revolution in the countryside. In this task the Liberation Army played a major role. The upheaval consisted of the confiscation of landlord holdings, the redistribution of the lands, and then subsequently the formation of agricultural cooperatives. From 1950 to 1954 army farms were established, later to be reorganized into military cooperatives. Late in 1954 those units engaged in economic construction were united in a special "production-construction army," and also put to work in industry. By the spring of 1956 agriculture had been so revolutionized that cooperatives were established throughout the Tarim Basin, where 80 percent of the peasant holdings were concentrated. The speed with which the transformation occurred may be realized from the following figures. Whereas in 1954 there were only 147 agricultural production cooperatives in Sinkiang, by July, 1956, there were altogether 10,781. After 1958, communes were established in the oases.

Not only were the sedentary peoples of Sinkiang affected by the revolution, but the nomadic tribes also were forced to modify their traditional patterns of living. As in the USSR and in the MPR, the Kazakh and Mongol pastoralists were settled onto large livestock farms. At the beginning of 1957 there were 629 pastoral producers' cooperatives, containing 24 percent of all herdsmen households. After that, communes were established in the pastoral areas, a development which caused some Sinkiang Kazakhs to migrate into the Soviet Union, where the regime seemed less oppressive. Such pressure forced the traditional felt yurt to yield to the "more progressive" mud or wooden house, which presumably was to precede the three or four-story stucco tenement, common throughout the Communist world.

In order to raise crop production in Sinkiang beyond the subsistence level, new areas were brought under cultivation. Improved and extended irrigation systems were constructed, both in the Tarim oases and in Dzhungaria, particularly along the Manass River. Composite expeditions of Soviet and Chinese scientists engaged in assessing irrigation potentials. Some of the new land was used to produce food; the rest went into cotton, Sinkiang's leading commercial crop. By 1960, Sinkiang produced 500,000 tons of grain, said to be more than enough for its population.

Elsewhere, along the southern borders of the MPR, the face of the land was under change. In Kansu a refinery was built to process the oil at Yumen, while a pipeline was laid to Lanchow where other refineries were scheduled to be put up.

In southeastern Inner Mongolia, as part of the plan to develop the industrial strength of the Northern Region centered on Peking, an iron and steel plant was completed at Paotow. When in operation (by 1962), it was to have a steel capacity of one million tons. In Kalgan and other nearby cities, new manufacturing establishments were built to produce mining equipment, textile machinery, and trucks. On the edge of the Gobi, reclamation projects, covering millions of acres of land and including the planting of extensive areas of forest shelter belts, were scheduled.

The industrialization and Sinification of Inner Mongolia were aided by new railways. In 1956 a rail line was opened between Ulan Bator and Tsining, thus linking Peking to the Trans-Siberian Railway across Inner and Outer Mongolia. And, from Paotow to Lanchow, paralleling the Hwang-Ho, another line was constructed.

RECENT DEVELOPMENTS IN THE MONGOLIAN PEOPLE'S REPUBLIC

Before 1945, when the MPR, isolated and cut off from the rest of the world, suffered under total Soviet domination, the Mongol economy made little progress toward providing a richer material life for the Mongol people. Although the sown area of the republic increased substantially during the war years primarily because the Soviets could not meet the basic grain needs of the Mongols, acreage again fell to near the prewar level in the immediate postwar period. Indeed, since there had been no industrial construction to speak of during the war, postwar Mongolia differed little from prewar Mongolia. The population had remained at less than 900,000, having grown from 759,200 in 1944 to 884,800 in 1958, with an overall density of about two persons per square mile so that livestock outnumbered the Mongols substantially (Table VIII).

On the surface, the Communist success in China seemed to have changed the situation dramatically for Mongolia. The MPR no longer constituted a buffer between the USSR and China, or a shield against attack on the USSR by Japan. Now, recognized as an independent entity in 1950 by Peking, Mongolia had become a territorial link between Moscow and Peking, joined by common ideology and aspirations.

Before the war the Soviet Union had been extremely niggardly in its assistance to Mongolia, probably because the Soviets could ill afford to give much while Mongolia itself was remote, exposed, and difficult to depend on in case of war. In these respects the small

TABLE VIII.

Livestock in the Mongolian People's Republic, 1958

Camels	864,000
Cattle	1,954,800
Goats	5,594,200
Horses	2,449,300
Sheep	12,579,900

Source: I. Kh. Ovidiyenko, *Sovremennaya mongoliya*, Moscow, 1964, p. 113.

republic was not unlike much of Eastern Siberia and the Soviet Far East. (The Soviets did assist in the construction of an industrial combine erected in Ulan Bator in 1934 to produce leather goods, shoes, etc.) For their part, the Mongols were incapable, through lack of trained labor and of other resources, of carrying out their own development program. However, in 1946, a beginning was made at speeding up growth, and the Mongols were assisted to a considerable degree by the Soviet Union. To a new ten-year treaty of friendship and mutual assistance with the MPR, there were added supplementary economic and cultural agreements. To improve communications a railroad was constructed south from Ulan-Ude on the Trans-Siberian to Ulan Bator, the capital of the Mongolian Republic. The ensuing five-year plan, 1948–52, brought with it some increase in agricultural production and a start in the modernization of the capital.

The next five-year plan (1953–57) witnessed a speed-up in development, especially as Chinese Communist assistance was now made available. In 1952 the CPR and the MPR signed a ten-year agreement for cultural and economic cooperation, while in 1955 arangements were made whereby Chinese labor could migrate under contract to Mongolia. A number of industrial enterprises were planned under the terms of these agreements, including the construction of a large woolen textile combine. Built by Chinese labor to specifications drafted by Soviet engineers with machinery purchased from Great Britain, this combine has since been put into operation. Additional agreements with the CPR on free aid and long-term credits were reached in 1956 and in 1958, while in 1957 the USSR undertook to aid Mongolia's three-year plan (1957–60) by extending new credits.

In 1954–55 the Mongol government embarked on another major effort to collectivize the livestock economy—this time with obviously more success. Before the end of 1959, it was reported, the whole herding population of about 650,000 had joined rural economy cooperatives, while about three-fourths of the country's livestock had been collectivized.[12] Another effort, too, was made to plough up the land, following the lead of the Khrushchev virgin and idle lands program, instituted in the spring of 1954. The Mongolian program, however, was nowhere near the proportions of the Soviet, which involved the ploughing of more than 70 million acres of land. The turning of the Mongol sod got off to a slow start, but further assistance rendered by the Soviets in a treaty in 1959 sped up the development. Under this agreement the Soviet Union supplied the Mongolian grain farms with caterpillar and other tractors as well as other farm equipment. In addition, Mongolian farm workers received the assistance of Soviet agricultural specialists. By 1959, the sown area had increased five times over 1954 and wheat production had grown reportedly 36 times, but total acreage involved remained relatively small. Dry farming cannot be practiced to any extent in Mongolia because of the light and unreliable precipitation. Even so, by 1961 Mongolia was said to be self-sufficient in cereals.[13]

[12] "Economic Advance in Mongolia," *The World Today*, Vol. 16, No. 6, June, 1960, p. 261.
[13] *Mongolia Today*, June–July, 1965, p. 2.

On the other hand, the irrigation potential, however small, had not been developed to any significant degree. The first major project, engineered with Chinese assistance, was the diversion of water from the Orkhon River to the Karakhoun State Farm near the site of Karakorum. (Though one of the largest irrigation projects in Mongolia, it never irrigated more than 40,000 acres in the region.)

This massive reorganization of Mongolian agriculture required careful preparation as well as considerable financial assistance from outside. Veterinary facilities were improved and a systematic campaign was waged against livestock disease. In the cooperatives themselves, of which there were about 389, schools were established as well as shops, cinemas, and medical centers. And, the yurt, too, began to yield to fixed communities of wooden houses or blocks of apartment houses.

The yurt, a round, low felt tent, ideally suited to conditions in Mongolia, is despised by the modern Mongol intellectual and party leader as a sign of backwardness. Nowhere was the struggle to replace the yurt with modern dwellings more apparent than in Ulan Bator, the industrial center of the republic and only city of any size. There, with Soviet and Chinese assistance, rows of new apartments began to rise along paved streets as Ulan Bator pressed toward the 20th century. Within a few years after much of the heavy construction work had been completed, the capital resembled most provincial Soviet cities. By far the most impressive structure, as of 1959, was the embassy of the Chinese People's Republic.

The industrial development of Ulan Bator and the general economic growth of Mongolia were accompanied by improvements in transport. The railway linking the city to the Trans-Siberian was extended southward in 1955 to the Chinese border to connect with a Chinese line running northward from Tsining to Erhlien on the border. Tsining is several hundred miles due west of Peking. The Chinese portion of the line, from Tsining to Ehrlien, was built in the same broad gauge as the Mongolian and Russian lines. Travelers on the railway reported that the trip into Mongolia either from the

USSR or from the CPR was made in broad gauge Russian cars, which were adaptable for use on the narrower Chinese gauge.[14] The extension of the route into China obviously did much to facilitate the dispatch of Chinese aid to the Mongols. It also encouraged the further exploitation of the coal fields south of Ulan Bator and the oil deposits near Sayn-Shanda in the Gobi, in southern Mongolia. Finally, the through railways truly made Mongolia a "corridor" and a link, rather than a dead-end street, with important implications.

In 1960–61, further agreements with the USSR and the CPR insured continued developmental progress for Mongolia. The May, 1960, Treaty of Friendship and Mutual Assistance with the CPR was accompanied by Agreements on Economic and Technical Aid and on Scientific and Technical Cooperation. Peking undertook to provide a long-term loan (1961–65) and assistance in the carrying out of new projects, including the construction of utilities and water conservancy measures. These agreements were followed in September, 1960, by another on Chinese labor in Mongolia. In the same month, the Soviets agreed also to provide additional aid, and in December they reached a new trade arrangement with Mongolia. Subsequently, in April, 1961, the USSR promised economic assistance to Mongolia's new five-year plan and this agreement was followed a week later by a new Chinese-Mongolian commercial treaty.

Mongolia's economic and cultural contacts were not confined to the USSR and the CPR only. The Czechs began to render assistance, establishing a modern shoe industry in Mongolia; the Hungarians sank wells; the East Germans provided a color printing plant; and Bulgaria gave agricultural assistance. (Economic relations with the Soviet-East European bloc were formalized finally in 1962 when the MPR joined CMEA, or COMECON, the Council for Mutual

---

[14] Klaus Mehnert, "Die Transmongolische Bahn und das Verhältnis Peking-Moskau," *Osteuropa,* Vol. VII, December, 1957, pp. 868–869.

Economic Assistance.) Foreign aid did much to bring Mongolia into the 20th century. As a consequence, gross industrial output, the Mongols claimed, increased 7.4 times between 1940 and 1960.

SUMMARY

The immediate postwar period was one of considerable confusion in the Chinese borderlands. Despite the accord between the Soviet regime and the Chinese Nationalists in 1945, the former did little to support the Nationalist cause in either Sinkiang or Manchuria. Indeed, the very reverse was true. The Red Army systematically looted the industrial plant of Manchuria before it withdrew, while in Sinkiang the Soviets played an all-too-familiar game. In that respect, the Kennan-Harriman telegram was highly prophetic.

In the following decade, that is from 1950 to 1960, Sino-Soviet relations reached a level of cooperation hitherto unknown in Russian and Chinese history. The Soviet regime finally withdrew from both Manchuria and Sinkiang, making possible the implementation of effective Chinese Communist control in those strategic territories. On the other hand, Soviet hegemony was preserved in Outer Mongolia, a fact which, tacitly, Peking must have acknowledged in its recognition of the independence of the MPR. With Soviet aid and assistance, the economies of both Manchuria and Sinkiang recovered and a foundation was laid for further growth. Joint Sino-Soviet pledges to the MPR, while suggesting some competitiveness between the two major powers, nevertheless revealed clearly the advantages open to Mongolia so long as the ideological ties prevailed and stability was maintained.

4 *The Problem of Western Interpretation of the Role of the Borderlands During the Period of Sino-Soviet Friendship*

THE NEW SITUATION IN ASIA

THE Chinese Communist Party, founded over forty years ago, was organized with support from the Communist Party of the Soviet Union. In the early years of the party's history there were miscalculations in tactics, some of which have been traced to the Soviet regime. The net result was that in 1927 the Chinese Communists were banished by the Nationalists to the countryside. There they were compelled to work out a new strategy for revolution under the leadership of Mao Tse-tung. They did not, however, disavow their Marxist ideological roots and ancestors. Nor did they deny the heritage of Lenin and Stalin, or their indebtedness to the Russian Communist Party. In the closing days of World War II and in the months that followed, with Red Army assistance and captured Japanese and American equipment, the Chinese Communists achieved a surprisingly quick victory in Manchuria, and shortly thereafter throughout the country. Indeed, the speed with which the revolution was carried out in 1949 may have surprised the Soviets as much as it shook the West and especially the United States, which had looked forward to a friendly alliance with postwar Nationalist China.

Out of the Communist revolution in China there seemed to emerge a new politico-geographical situation in Asia, the implications of which were not fully seen in the West. For Soviet Russia and Communist China, linked by a common ideology, shared above all the goal of world communism to which, and on which, all other objectives were assumed to be subordinate and dependent. Yet the close state relationships or, as some Western observers termed it, the axis partnership that developed between Moscow and Peking, symbolized a significant break with history.[1] For the record of Russo-Chinese relationships over past centuries had demonstrated mounting Russian pressure against a weakening China in the struggle over border territories.

Indeed, the expansion of Russia across Asia from the 17th century on had been largely at the expense of the Chinese Empire, however vague and undefined outer limits of the Empire may have been. As the Russian drive gained momentum after the middle of the 19th century, it led to the imposition of a series of treaties and agreements on China, which confirmed the seizure of territory in the Far East, of the Mongolian plateau, and of extensive steppe lands in Inner Asia. In addition to what the tsars incorporated into their empire, there were serious efforts to annex other Chinese border territories or gain wherever possible some economic advantage.

Though the Ch'ing emperors had been overlords of Manchuria, Outer and Inner Mongolia, much of Turkestan, and of Tibet, they were never able to administer these territories effectively. Except for Manchuria and to a lesser extent Inner Mongolia, the border regions remained ethnically non-Chinese. And in spite of the Sinification of Manchuria, and again to a lesser degree of Inner Mongolia, foreign influence whether Russian or Japanese was often more decisive than Chinese. This situation was equally true of Sinkiang because of its great distance from China proper.

---

[1] Howard L. Boorman and others, *Moscow-Peking Axis: Strengths and Strains,* New York: Harper & Bros., 1957, 227 pp.

By the end of the 19th century the Russians were well on their way to dominating northern and central Manchuria by their construction and control of the Chinese Eastern Railway. Russian hegemony over Manchuria, however, was effectively challenged by the Japanese, who were victorious in the Russo-Japanese War of 1904. Thereafter Japan moved into the ascendancy although, by agreement, mutual Russo-Japanese spheres of interest were created in the rich province. Thirteen years later, the Bolshevik Revolution —and the ensuing chaos in Russia—helped to clear the way for the realization of Japan's ambitions in East Asia, which reached their apogee in the 1930's when Manchuria became Manchukuo, a Japanese puppet state. At the same time, Japanese interest and influence in Inner Mongolia further weakened whatever remained of Chinese control over the eastern Gobi after the establishment over a decade before of a Soviet-protected Mongolian People's Republic to the north.

Similarly, central Chinese influence was reduced in Sinkiang to the point where the territory was virtually self-governing, though within the Soviet sphere. When the Chinese Nationalists were at last in a position to take over the administration of the remote province after the Red Army had been withdrawn because of the war in Eastern Europe, they were unable to accomplish much. Internal disorders among the Turkic peoples, partly encouraged by Moscow, the struggle against Japan in the east, and later the civil war hampered Nationalist authorities and prevented effective control.

The Communist Revolution in China thus marked a new era, not only for China proper but also for the borderlands—Manchuria, Sinkiang, Inner Mongolia, and Outer Mongolia. The sharing of a common ideology between Moscow and Peking seemed at last to have brought a degree of stability to these vital provinces, a stability which hitherto had been lacking. It was for this reason that whatever boundary differences there were between Russia and China and China and the MPR in evidence on Sino-Soviet maps were not regarded as of sufficient importance to disturb the new alliance. The goals of international communism were believed to be of a scale far outweighing rather limited cartographic discrepancies. Indeed, nowhere in the early years of the ideological friendship did either the Russians or the Chinese Communists refer officially and publicly to any boundary problem. Even Chinese Communist maps showed the historic settlements on the left bank of the Amur, near the mouth of the Zeya, as being within the USSR, despite the fact that the Nationalists on Taiwan continued to insist on Chinese ownership.

Right up until the Chinese Communist success in Manchuria and Sinkiang, the Soviet regime had intended to make these strategic territories dependent on, if not a part of, the USSR. This goal undoubtedly accounted for the systematic stripping of Manchurian industry by the Red Army. Clearly Nationalist China was to be kept in a relatively weaker position. The objective of Soviet policy thus explains Russian interference in the affairs of Sinkiang while the Nationalists, with whom by treaty Moscow was allied, were preoccupied elsewhere with the forces of Mao Tse-tung. At any rate the Communist success in China compelled a reassessment of Soviet policy. Even so, the withdrawal of the Soviets from Manchuria and Sinkiang was not immediate. Indeed, in the negotiation of the Treaty of Friendship and Mutual Assistance in 1950, Stalin had pressed excessive demands on Mao. Nevertheless, Moscow promised to compensate China for the machines and installations seized in Manchuria and to permit the unification of China and its borderlands under Peking. Five years later Soviet forces were returned to the USSR, an act regarded as having major significance, for this was a withdrawal for which little precedent may be found in Russian history. But this was a surrender not to Japan nor to Nationalist China, but to comrades in the international struggle, to Communist China. Moscow, therefore in effect gave its stamp of approval to the ultimate Sinification of the border provinces of China with the implication that henceforth Soviet influence there would be kept to a minimum.

If ideology is to be taken as the essential link between Russia and China, traditional national interests—which under ordinary circumstances might have caused friction—have to be thought of as having only secondary importance. As Donald Treadgold noted:

It is not at all clear that the Communist totalitarian states . . . ought to be considered as essentially similar in structure and behavior to nation-states as nineteenth- and early twentieth-century international relations conceived of them. Of course the external structure of nationhood remains, and is useful to the Communists in that part of their activities where they operate within recognized and accepted international organizations and relationships. . . . [However, it is not necessary to state] that the older idea of nation-state is irrelevant to international Communism but only that it is insufficient to explain either the domestic policies and practices of Communist governments . . . or the expansion of the international Communist movement beyond Communist-ruled countries. . . .[2]

If viewed in this manner the rebirth of the powerful Manchurian industrial base under Chinese Communist direction could not have been regarded by Moscow as a threat to its hold on Trans-Baykalia and the Maritime province. In turn, Russian plans to promote the more rapid economic growth of Eastern Siberia had to be assessed essentially in the context of domestic territorial objectives, rather than as a concerted effort to insure that these remote territories remain Russian. And the announcement of joint Sino-Soviet plans for the development and utilization of the water resources of the Amur Basin further strengthened the thesis that a stability, hitherto lacking, would be reflected in further economic advance in the

[2] Donald W. Treadgold, "Russia and the Far East," in *Russian Foreign Policy: Essays in Historical Perspective*, Ivo J. Lederer (ed.), New Haven: Yale University Press, 1962, pp. 573–574.

border provinces. Finally, the construction of railway links—and, indeed, the improvement of communications generally—between Russia and China through Mongolia and Sinkiang had to be construed as part of the joint effort to strengthen the power base of international Communism. Thus, the fact of the Eurasian landmass between East Berlin and Hanoi lying within the grip of a monolithic hostile movement was for much of the Western world during the 1950's a frightening reality.

ZONE OF PEACEFUL CONTACT OR POTENTIAL CONFLICT?

Despite the very strong (and official) evidence of inter-party unity under the leadership of Moscow, there were in the 1950's certain developments which showed not only that differences of opinion existed within the bloc but, as events in Hungary dramatically revealed, there was even a willingness to fight rather than continue to submit to Stalinism. Despite the apparent stability in the Sino-Soviet borderlands, there was evidence that the rivalries of the past had not been eliminated.

The speed with which the Chinese Communists implemented their nationalities policy, for example, suggested that Peking was determined to liquidate both native autonomy movements and any Soviet encouragement of them. A cause for greater speculation, however, was the extremely ambiguous position of the Mongolian People's Republic.

In return for their postwar recognition of the independence of the MPR, the Chinese Nationalists were promised Soviet assistance in their efforts to unify and restore the republic, long ravaged by war. When it became clear that Stalin had no intention of living up to the 1945 agreement, and in fact seemed determined to keep China weak, the Nationalists withdrew their recognition of Ulan Bator and thereafter for many years blocked the admission of Mongolia to the United Nations.

When the Chinese Communists in 1950 extended recognition to

the MPR, the act seemed more than anything else an acknowledgment of Soviet hegemony over the small republic, an acceptance of the status quo. But over the long run Chinese Communist acceptance of Mongolian independence was difficult to reconcile with the implied objectives of Mao Tse-tung. These had been related in a general way to Edgar Snow in 1936, when the latter met the Chinese leader in his hideout in Yenan. Mao had indicated, according to Snow, that when the people's revolution had been victorious in China, the Outer Mongolian Republic would automatically become a part of the Chinese federation.[3] Mao had added "at their own will," but the impression was established that a Communist China would encompass not only the dominant Han, but also those ethnic groups which had been historically associated with the Chinese, principally the Mongols, Tibetans, and Turkis.

The establishment by the Chinese Communists in Ulan Bator early in the 1950's of an embassy on a scale more appropriate to a major world capital strengthened further the impression that Peking intended to play a significant role in Outer Mongolia. The construction of a rail link between China and Outer Mongolia, the granting of economic aid and assistance at a time when the Chinese mainland itself was undergoing reconstruction, and the movement northward of thousands of Chinese laborers accompanied by wives and children, with the promise of ultimate MPR citizenship—all encouraged the belief that Peking intended to challenge Moscow's preeminent position on the plateau. Undoubtedly, it was such considerations as these which prompted George Kennan in 1961 to wonder ". . . how long Russia will be able to retain her hegemony in Outer Mongolia now that the alternative is not Japanese power but the power of China itself." [4]

Apart from the speculation that arose in the West over possible

---

[3] Edgar Snow, *Red Star over China*, New York: Random House, 1938, p. 96 (footnote).

[4] *Atlantic Monthly*, May, 1961, p. 36.

Sino-Soviet rivalry in the borderlands, there were those who believed that whatever the professions of ideological solidarity, a conflict was inevitable between the USSR and the CPR stemming from China's bulging population and the need for *lebensraum*. Those who subscribed to this thesis drew heavily on the writing of Wilhelm Starlinger.

He was a German physician who spent five years in a Soviet concentration camp at the end of World War II and came in contact with prisoners from all parts of the Soviet Union. His discussions with the other inmates led him to the conclusion that as a result of China's rapidly growing population, outlets would have to be provided in the Soviet Far East and in Outer Mongolia, as well as in Southeast Asia. And, moreover, Starlinger believed that the Soviet regime was aware of this danger.[5]

Starlinger's conclusions, despite a certain logic, were based on very superficial evidence. Still his writing had considerable influence on geopolitical thinking in both France and West Germany.

Harrison Salisbury, a correspondent for *The New York Times,* formerly stationed in Moscow and a more acute observer of Soviet affairs than Starlinger, also anticipated future conflict. "For it is perfectly apparent," Salisbury wrote, "to anyone who reads the statistics (i.e., of China's population growth), that [there] . . . are going to be heavy and continuous population pressures on those great vacant lands of Russia's to the East (lands, incidentally, which in most cases were at one time the property of China). . . ."[6]

Salisbury considered the Khrushchev virgin and idle land program —a program which in the latter half of the 1950's resulted in the ploughing of millions of acres of little used land in western Siberia and northern Kazakhstan, and the subsequent settling of several

---

[5] John E. Tashjean, *Where China Meets Russia: An Analysis of Dr. Starlinger's Theory,* Central Asian Collectanea, No. 2, Washington, D.C., 67 pp.

[6] Harrison E. Salisbury, *To Moscow—and Beyond,* New York: Harper & Bros., 1959, p. 249.

hundred thousand Russians and Ukrainians—proof of Soviet concern for its vast empty Siberian spaces.

Unquestionably the Khrushchev program was motivated politically, but more compelling reasons for its implementation could be found in domestic conditions—namely, the grain problem—than in the Chinese population problem. The Soviet Far East, it is true, is sparsely settled and man-land ratios are low. Crop cultivation there, however, is confined by a short growing season and permafrost to relatively small areas of good soil in the Amur-Ussuri lowland. Greater densities undoubtedly can be achieved, but industrialization rather than agricultural development may be the key. As an outlet for China's peasantry, the region offers little.

Nor is it conceivable that the high, semi-arid plateau of Mongolia, where the irrigation potential remains relatively low, could support a substantial increase in population, at least under present technology. At any rate, Chinese peasant colonization in Mongolia probably would not in any way relieve the congestion in China proper.

Despite the growth in the Chinese population, not all observers in the West saw this increase necessarily as a problem that was destined to disrupt Sino-Soviet relations. Among those who took issue with the population overflow thesis was Karl August Wittfogel, a more serious student of Chinese history than either Starlinger or Salisbury. Indeed, Wittfogel came to the conclusion that the Chinese population problem was not one of excess so much as of shortage of labor in the countryside. What Starlinger and Salisbury failed to take into account was the effect of collectivization on traditional Chinese farming. China did not have a surplus population, but, Wittfogel noted, due to the reorganization in farming, suffered a very real shortage of workers, a shortage likely to persist during the next "historical" period.[7] China's problem, accordingly, was not

[7] Karl A. Wittfogel, "Demography," in *Bear and Dragon: What Is the Relation between Moscow and Peking?* James Burham (ed.), New York: National Review, Inc., 1960, pp. 33–36.

to seek foreign outlets for its growing population but to find ways of raising productivity in the communes.

The Wittfogel thesis, however, tended to beg the question. By what means are the Chinese Communists to raise the productivity of the countryside where, under historic systems of land management—particularly in irrigated regions—yields have traditionally been high? Has the loss of population to the cities necessarily meant a loss of labor in the countryside and thus a decline in output?

Finally, whatever conclusions Western observers may have reached concerning the Chinese population, the official Peking Communist Party line throughout the 1950's generally viewed the notion of overpopulation as a myth generated by Malthusian reactionaries in order to conceal the true cause of human misery, namely capitalism.[8] According to Friedrich Engels, it was noted in Communist China, "if Malthus had not considered the matter so one-sidedly, he could not have failed to see that surplus population or labor power is invariably tied up with surplus wealth, surplus capital, and surplus landed property." [9] Thus, it was said in Peking,

After people have freed themselves from heavy fetters and established a socialist system, they become the masters of land and machine; pursuing self-conscious labor, instead of being compelled to work; and a large population becomes a very important factor in promoting rapid development of the national economy and culture. Under such circumstances, the larger the population is, the greater, faster, better, and more economic will be socialist construction; the faster will a nation become rich and strong, with the people enjoying a higher level of material and cultural life.[10]

[8] Kingsley Davis, "The Political Impact of New Population Trends," *Foreign Affairs,* January, 1958, p. 293.

[9] Quoted in *Hsin Chien-she* (New Construction), No. 5, Peking, May, 1960, pp. 1–13.

[10] *Ibid.,* pp. 14–19.

Despite such optimism, the regime did in more realistic moods occasionally hint that it was not unmindful of the problems posed by too rapid an increase. Thus the party newspaper, *People's Daily,* in 1957 warned of the need for birth control. Stating that China's population was growing by more than 13 million a year, the *Daily* argued that economic development could not keep up with this rapid surge in numbers. Its recommendation—the discouragement of early marriages! [11]

SUMMARY

Western speculation notwithstanding, it seems clear that no one in the Free World fully appreciated the extent to which Peking was concerned about its border territories, nor the strength of its interest in the Mongolian question. It was not until 1964, after the Sino-Soviet dispute had reached the proportions of a "cold war," that the Chinese position became evident. In that year, in the course of a meeting between Mao and a delegation of the Japanese Socialist Party, the Chinese leader revealed the nature of the claims against the Soviet Union. Speaking on Outer Mongolia, Mao stated that "when Khrushchev and Bulganin came to China (in 1954), we took up this question but they refused to talk to us. . . ." [12]

The Chinese position was in turn confirmed by *Pravda* in September, 1964, when the Soviet newspaper reported that Peking had demanded Soviet permission to reincorporate Mongolia into China, on the basis that it was not really an independent country.[13] Finally, *A Short History of Modern China,* published in Peking in 1954 but not widely known in the West until later, contained an illustration not only showing Outer Mongolia as an integral part of China, but outlining those territories in Asia lost by China over

[11] Davis, *op. cit.*
[12] Reported in *The New York Times,* September 10, 1964.
[13] *Ibid.*

a century before, namely the Soviet Far East, the Pamirs, the Semirechiye, and the peninsulas of Southeast Asia.[14]

With the advantages of hindsight, it becomes increasingly evident that in the early 1960's very real issues pertaining to the state were no longer lying dormant but had come to the surface and were a factor in Sino-Soviet relations even before the ideological dispute. The dispute, however, tended to exacerbate the competition for influence or control in the borderlands.

[14] Dennis J. Doolin, *Territorial Claims in the Sino-Soviet Conflict. Documents and Analyses,* Hoover Institution Studies: 7, Stanford, 1965, pp. 16, 43.

5   *The Borderlands and the Sino-Soviet Dispute*

ALTHOUGH certain differences of opinion between Moscow and Peking had existed since 1950 (and reportedly between the Soviet and Chinese Communist Parties before that), none of these had led to an open break. Nor were any of these differences aired publicly. Consequently when in 1959 the notion of a falling out between the two Communist powers became widespread in Western capitals, there was a tendency to disregard the possibility of an open break.

The desire to see the development of friction within the Communist bloc—or to see Moscow's monolithic position challenged—was a legitimate one, but there were obvious dangers for the West if too much importance were attached to press reports of verbal disagreements. Moreover, in both Moscow and Peking, efforts were made to minimize the differences; rumors circulating in the Western World were described simply as gossip.[1] Indeed, Mao Tse-tung even described reported differences with Moscow as "non-antogonistic; and such differences," he noted, "not only do not hinder (Sino-Soviet) cooperation, but, on the contrary, stimulate progress."[2] With that, one Western observer was compelled to write: "It may seem paradoxical to state the truth that the leaders of China and

[1] *The New York Times,* July 9, 1961.
[2] Wlodzimierz Baczkowski, "World History," in *Bear and Dragon: What Is the Relation between Moscow and Peking?* James Burnham (ed.), New York: National Review, Inc., 1960, pp. 9–13.

Russia differ not in matters that divide them, but in matters that unite them." [3]

The Western World, of course, is now aware that many of the inconsistencies in Chinese Communist and Soviet Russian statements were, in reality, a reflection of the troubled state of affairs that pursued the Sino-Soviet relationship. The Khrushchev de-Stalinization program, followed by his criticism in 1958–59 of Peking's efforts to force the peasantry into communes [4] prompted the Chinese Communist leaders to make clear that the new China "was not obliged to follow in the footsteps of the Russians." [5]

In his own right, Mao was a Marxist-Leninist who had successfully brought about a revolution, following a long period of banishment in the countryside where, applying a logic that was non-Marxist, he had fashioned a party and created an elite. The Soviet leaders, with almost forty years of revolution behind them, appeared to the Chinese Communists to be too prone to sit down and discuss international problems with the West, as best instanced in the Khrushchev-Eisenhower Camp David talks in September, 1959. Still it was the Sino-Indian border war in August, 1959, that revealed how conservative the Soviet position on war and revolution had become. "One cannot fail to express regret," Tass, the Soviet news agency, commented, "at the fact that the incident on the Sino-Indian frontier took place. The Soviet Union is on friendly relations both with the Chinese People's Republic and the Republic of India. . . ." [6]

Some years later, in February, 1963, the Peking *People's Daily* noted that it was this Soviet statement that first brought "the internal differences among the fraternal parties . . . into the open.

[3] *Ibid.*

[4] David Floyd, *Mao Against Khrushchev. A Short History of the Sino-Soviet Conflict,* New York: Praeger, 1963, p. 63.

[5] Robert C. North, "The Sino-Soviet Alliance," *The China Quarterly,* No. 1, Jan.–Mar., 1960, p. 56.

[6] Floyd, *op. cit.,* pp. 261–262.

. . . Making no distinction between right and wrong, the (Soviet) statement expressed 'regret' over the border clash and in reality condemned China's correct stand. . . ." [7]

In addition to these issues, the Sino-Soviet relationship was weakened by the nature of Soviet financial and economic aid to the People's Republic. The time was fast coming to an end when Peking could boast, as it did in 1955, that "the Soviet Union has extended a great deal of financial aid to our country both by a succession of loans granted us on the most favorable terms and by trade, selling us technical equipment and materials at low prices." [8]

Though the full amount of Soviet aid to Peking has never been revealed, the latter reportedly received between 1949 and 1957 loans totalling $2.2 billion. [9] The Soviets were committed to helping in the construction of over two hundred industrial plants in China and, from August, 1958 to February, 1959, agreed to help with an additional seventy-eight plants. Still, Soviet aid to Communist China on a per capita basis was less than that accorded some of the more subservient East European satellites. Moreover, reflecting its policy of assistance to select neutralist, lesser-developed countries, the Soviet Union had made larger loans to the United Arab Republic and to Iraq than to its socialist Chinese ally.

Whatever the reasons, including concern for Peking's militaristic stance and deep-seated fear of China's potential industrial power and influence, Soviet economic aid to China was sharply reduced in 1960. Not only were a large number of Soviet technicians in China recalled to Moscow, but the withdrawal of Soviet assistance caused Peking to radically alter its economic plans, already off-balance because of the failure of the "Great Leap Forward" in 1958. Nonetheless, in 1960 one Soviet writer asserted that:

[7] *Ibid.*, pp. 374–385.
[8] *Ibid.*, pp. 225–227.
[9] For a useful account of Sino-Soviet economic relations, see William E. Griffith, *The Sino-Soviet Rift*, Cambridge: The M.I.T. Press, 1964, pp. 231 ff.

the economic relations between the USSR and the CPR are weighted in favor of China, since the Soviet Union, which was first in taking the road to socialist construction, has a more powerful economy, a more highly developed science and technology, and greater experience in the construction of socialism. On the other hand, as it implements effective socialist reorganization and a rapid development of the economy of the country, the CPR gives even greater help to the Soviet Union by sharing with it the valuable experience of many centuries . . . and by supplying the USSR with some useful minerals, various manufactures, and rare subtropical products . . . to the benefit of Communist construction in our country.[10]

THE ISSUE OF THE UNEQUAL TREATIES

Despite the worsening of Sino-Soviet relations, the bloc countries continued to function as if little of unusual significance were taking place. On December 23, 1962, a Sino-Mongolian boundary agreement was signed in Peking. The presence of the Mongolian premier, Yumshagin Tsedenbal, in the Chinese capital afforded the then mayor of Peking, Peng Chen, an opportunity to proclaim that "all problems between Communist countries should be solved in accordance with the principles of Marxism-Leninism and the principles guiding relations between fraternal countries laid down in the (1957) Moscow statement and the (1960) Moscow declaration." [11] However, Khrushchev's speech on foreign policy to the Supreme Soviet on December 12th had—once again—treaded on Chinese sensitivities.

Irritated by Chinese Communist criticism of the Soviet handling of the Cuban crisis, Khrushchev saw fit to remind Peking that two remnants of colonialism, namely Macao and Hong Kong, remained on the south coast of China.

[10] M. I. Sladkovskiy, "Sovetsko-kitayskoye ekonomicheskoye sotrudnicheskoye," *Problemy vostokovedeniya*, No. 3, July, 1960, pp. 108–117.
[11] *The London Times,* December 24, 1962.

But no one will denounce the Chinese People's Republic for leaving intact these fragments of colonialism [he said]. It would be wrong to prod China into any kind of actions which she considers untimely. If the government of the Chinese People's Republic tolerates Macao and Hong Kong, it clearly has good reasons for doing so. Therefore, it would be ridiculous to level against it the accusation that this is a concession to Britain and Portuguese colonialists, that this is appeasement.

But maybe this is a retreat from Marxism-Leninism? Nothing of the kind. It means that the government of the Chinese People's Republic takes into account the realities, the actual possibilities. . . .[12]

Bristling at Khrushchev's references to the colonial enclaves on China's southern coast, the *People's Daily* retaliated in March, 1963, with a defense of the Chinese attitude toward the Cuban crisis, airing publicly for the first time the question of the loss of territory to Imperial Russia in the 19th century (Figure 7).

For us there never has been a question of a "double standard." We have only one standard, whether in dealing with the questions of Taiwan, whether in dealing with the questions of Hong Kong and Macao, or whether dealing with all international questions, and that standard is Marxism-Leninism, proletarian internationalism, the interests of the Chinese people and of the people of the world, the interests of world peace and the revolutionary cause of the people of all countries. . . . Inasmuch as some persons have mentioned . . . Hong Kong and Macao, we are obliged to discuss a little of the history of imperialist aggressions against China.

In the hundred years or so prior to the victory of the Chinese revolution, the imperialist and colonial powers—the United States, Britain, France, Tsarist Russia, Germany, Japan, Italy, Austria, Belgium, the Netherlands, Spain and Portugal—carried out unbridled aggression against China. They compelled the governments of old China to sign

---

[12] Floyd, *op. cit.,* pp. 327–333. See also Dennis J. Doolin, *Territorial Claims in the Sino-Soviet Conflict. Documents and Analyses,* Hoover Institution Studies: 7, Stanford, 1965, pp. 19, 27–28.

a large number of unequal treaties: the Treaty of Nanking in 1842, the Treaty of Aigun in 1858, the Treaty of Tientsin in 1858, the Treaty of Peking in 1860, the Treaty of Ili of 1881, the Protocol of Lisbon of 1887, the Treaty of Shimonoseki of 1895, the Convention for the Extension of Hong Kong of 1898, the Treaty of 1901, etc. By virtue of these unequal treaties, they annexed Chinese territory in the north, south, east and west and held leased territories on the seaboard and in the hinterland of China. . . .

At the time the People's Republic of China was inaugurated, our government declared that it would examine the treaties concluded by previous Chinese governments with foreign governments, treaties that had been left over by history, and would recognize, abrogate, revise or renegotiate them according to their respective contents. . . .

We know very well, and you know too, that you are, to put it plainly, bringing up the questions of Hong Kong and Macao merely as a fig-leaf to hide your disgraceful performance in the Caribbean crisis. . . .[13]

The Soviet retreat in the confrontation with the United States over Cuba provided the immediate background for the injection of the question of China's lost territories into the Sino-Soviet dispute. To be sure, Communist Chinese cartographic descriptions of the Sino-Soviet boundary had not coincided in every sector with those of Soviet Russia. And Peking had not, since the early 1950's at least, considered the status of Outer Mongolia as final. The unrest among the minorities, demonstrated by events in Sinkiang, clearly showed that Chinese control of the province was less than total and Soviet influence remained a factor to be dealt with. Still, the Communist Chinese reference to the "unequal treaties"—imposed by an Imperial Russia on an Imperial China—was to further complicate Sino-Soviet relations.

The "unequal treaties" with Imperial Russia, to which the Chinese Communists referred, were (1) the Treaty of Aigun; (2) the Treaty of Peking; and (3) the Treaty of Ili or St. Petersburg. Earlier

[13] *The New York Times,* March 9, 19, 22, 1963; Floyd, *op. cit.,* pp. 388–390.

treaties with Russia, such as Nerchinsk in 1689—which drew the Russo-Chinese boundary in East Asia along the Stanovoy Mountains—and Kiakhta in 1727—which initiated the delineation of the boundary between Siberia and Outer Mongolia—were not questioned. The three 19th-century treaties were, in truth, imposed by an expanding Russia on a weakening Manchu Dynasty, treaties which the Chinese had to accept. The legal status of the 19th-century treaties remains unchanged. However, Peking's exhumation of past grievances represents undoubtedly a source of considerable embarrassment for Moscow, if only because it tends to link the Soviet regime with tsarist imperialism.

THE KARAKHAN DECLARATION

Following their seizure of power in 1917, the Bolsheviks—in effective control of little more than Central Russia—were inclined to disassociate themselves from the imperial policies of the Romanovs. Indeed, in an appeal to the Chinese people on July 25, 1919, L. M. Karakhan, the Assistant Commissar of Foreign Affairs, renounced on behalf of the new Soviet regime all tsarist conquests in China, Manchuria, and other regions, Russia's share in the Boxer indemnity, together with all the special privileges enjoyed by Russian merchants in China.[14] The renunciation of these rights, Karakhan suggested, could be written into a treaty which would abolish all acts of force and injustice.

The declaration brought no immediate response from the Chinese, but its intent did have a favorable impact generally on China. Shortly thereafter Chinese receptiveness to Soviet overtures was confirmed in what was then described as the first "equal" treaty between China and a foreign power, the Agreement on General Principles, signed in Peking in May, 1924. In the treaty the Russians and Chinese agreed to establish diplomatic relations and joint ad-

---

[14] Louis Fischer, *The Soviets in World Affairs,* Princeton: Princeton University Press, 1951, Vol. II, pp. 538–550.

ministration of the Chinese Eastern Railway (pending a final arrangement to be made at a later conference). The Soviet Union, for its part, recognized China's sovereignty over Outer Mongolia and surrendered the special rights and privileges obtained through the earlier unequal treaties. The purpose of the Karakhan Declaration had been somewhat vague. Karakhan had not renounced those former Imperial Chinese territories incorporated into the Russian Empire by the tsars. Moreover, in spite of the friendly overtures to China, subsequent Soviet policy in reality differed little from that of the Russian tsars toward the Manchus. From 1921 to 1927, while the Soviet leaders attempted to promote Communism in China, they made efforts coincidentally to regain and strengthen Russian influence in the borderlands. Though the Japanese succeeded in edging the Russians out of Manchuria and obtaining control of the vital railway, the Soviets were singularly successful in establishing *de facto* control over Outer Mongolia, which became the Mongolian People's Republic, and in penetrating economically the province of Sinkiang (specifically, Dzhungaria) following the completion of the Turk-Sib Railway.

In a recent issue of the Soviet publication, *International Life,* the Karakhan Declaration is recalled and an effort is made to reject Chinese claims to lost territories.[15] The fact that the statement was allowed to be published may provide some evidence of the concern Moscow feels for its Asian territories. The author, V. Khvostov, argues vigorously that the Chinese reference to the unequal treaties is designed to inflame hatred and represents a politically intolerable position for a true Marxist-Leninist Party. The unequal treaties were abrogated by the Soviet leaders after the Revolution, but, according to Khvostov, *these treaties were not concerned with the Russian-Chinese frontiers.* (Italics mine.) Rather, they referred to

[15] V. Khvostov in *Mezhdunarodnaya Zhizn,* No. 10, October, 1964, quoted in the *Central Asian Review,* Vol. XIII, No. 1, 1965, pp. 89–93.

those imposed by Imperial Japan on China, such as the Treaty of Shimonoseki in 1896, the Protocol of 1901, and subsequent agreements between 1907–1916.

The writer points out that the Chinese question the Soviet Union's right to more than one and one-half million square kilometers of territory. But *the nations within Russia's historical boundaries were liberated by the October Revolution* and united voluntarily within the framework of the RSFSR and, later, of the USSR. Many nations preferred union with Russia rather than face the Chinese threat. That applies equally, says Khvostov, to nations in the east (Lake Baykal and the Far East), which are predominantly Russian, as well as those in Central Asia.

While chiding the Chinese for having acquired their empire by conquest, Khvostov notes that to the west of the present Sino-Soviet Central Asian boundary the Chinese did have watch towers and pickets, but their political influence, historically, took the form of little more than plundering raids. Dzhungaria, for instance, became Chinese only in the mid-18th century when troops of the Manchu Dynasty liquidated the Dzhungarian khanate and "slaughtered more than a million natives."

BORDER VIOLATIONS AND
MINORITY UNREST IN SINKIANG

The growing dissonance in Sino-Soviet relations has been marked by unrest in Sinkiang and by periodic border violations and clashes between Russian and Chinese personnel both in Central Asia and in the Far East.

With the Communist Revolution in China, disturbances among the Turkic and other non-Han minorities in Sinkiang did not come to an end; there was simply less heard of them in the West. Despite a carefully constructed program during the 1950's of Sinification and political orientation aimed at the native peoples, they remained anti-Chinese and disaffected. Attempts to get the nomadic peoples to settle down in collectives, followed late in 1958 with the accelerated establishment of communes, drastically threatened traditional patterns of existence.[16]

The considerable economic distress which these programs provoked became more acute with the cancellation of Soviet economic aid and the withdrawal in 1960 of Soviet technicians from Sinkiang. Repressive measures taken by the Chinese regime against Soviet-oriented groups in order to reduce Soviet influence enhanced the anxiety and frustration of some of the native peoples. This in turn provoked further disturbances, culminating in flight to the Soviet Union. From the early months of 1962 onward, the migration became a full-scale exodus. Between April and August, 1962, some 60,000 Kazakhs, especially from the Ili Valley, reportedly crossed into Soviet Kazakhstan and were promptly settled on collective farms. Though Sinkiang Kazakhs seemed to have been the major element in the migration, Uighurs and other peoples fled also, principally into the Kirgiz and Tadzhik Republics.

The full extent of the distress did not become known in the West immediately. In March, 1963, came the Communist Chinese statement on the unequal treaties, followed in September by accusations of Russian subversion in Sinkiang.

. . . In April and May 1962 [claimed Peking] the leaders of the CPSU used their organs and personnel in Sinkiang, China, to carry out large-scale subversive activities in the Ili region and enticed and coerced several tens of thousands of Chinese citizens into going to the Soviet Union. The Chinese Government lodged repeated protests . . . but the Soviet Government refused to repatriate these Chinese citizens on the pretext of the "sense of Soviet legality" and "humanitarianism." [17]

Shortly thereafter a Soviet version of the problem appeared in *Pravda*. The latter noted that since 1960 the Chinese had been

[16] For an excellent account of the land reform, see George Moseley, *A Sino-Soviet Cultural Frontier,* East Asian Research Center, Harvard University, 1966, esp. pp. 42 ff.
[17] Griffith, *op. cit.,* p. 173.

"systematically violating the Soviet frontier" and that in 1962 alone "more than 5,000 such violations had occurred." *Pravda* further reported that the Chinese were trying illegally to annex disputed territory at the confluence of the Amur and Ussuri Rivers. Military retaliation was threatened if violations continued.[18]

Finally, in press reports directed at her own Central Asian minorities, Moscow charged that Chinese frontier guards had fired on the refugees, while eye-witness accounts recorded Chinese persecution in Sinkiang.[19]

The bitterness of these exchanges was heightened by the Naushki incident of September 12, 1962. Naushki, a border station on the Mongolian-Siberian Railway, lies to the south of Ulan-Ude. There, on the Peking-Moscow Express, Soviet border guards confiscated what was described as anti-Soviet propaganda, which the Chinese passengers, reportedly, were attempting to smuggle into Russia.[20] Peking protested the incident and, having already closed Soviet consulates in Shanghai, Dairen, Mukden, Urumchi, and Kuldja, now placed restrictions on the entry of Soviet citizens into Sinkiang. The Soviets in turn expelled Chinese citizens resident in Moscow.

During the same month, the Chinese Communists sent one million youths into the Northwest, ostensibly to cultivate virgin lands, but more likely to strengthen border defenses.

The tension continued through 1964. In June, on the occasion of the 100th anniversary of its "accession to Russia," the Soviet Kirgiz Republic was awarded the Order of Lenin. In September, the Soviet regime accused the Chinese of anti-Soviet activities in the USSR, financed through a trade in opium.[21] Continued Chinese persecution of the Turkic minorities in Sinkiang prompted *Sotsialistik Kazakhstan,* the Kazakh language newspaper in Alma-Ata, to charge that Chinese policy toward the Uighurs and Kazakhs was

---

[18] *Ibid.*
[19] *The New York Times,* October 13, 20, 1964.
[20] Griffith, *op. cit.,* pp. 174–176.
[21] *The New York Times,* September 14, 1964.

one of "great-power chauvinism." The newspaper, moreover, described the Chinese acquisition of Sinkiang in the 18th century "as a forcible enslavement of the peoples" and "subjugation to a most severe national-colonial yoke." For Marxists to state that people are subject to "colonial" rule, commented *The New York Times,* is to mark them as candidates for national liberation! [22]

The continuing polemic between the two Communist states led to rumors and unconfirmed reports of troop movements along the Sino-Soviet frontier. China's growing arsenal of nuclear weapons was an element of considerable concern to the Soviet Union.[23] To meet the challenge, the Russians reportedly transferred special intelligence units and equipment to border regions to monitor Chinese tests of missiles and nuclear warheads. Such units may have focused previously on United States military activities. In high level talks, therefore, Russian officials informed their U.S. counterparts that though they felt that none of the border disputes with China was worth a war, there was always the danger that neither would be willing to back off from a small border clash. Such clashes could escalate and lead to a nuclear explosion.

By early 1967 a new element had entered the scene, increasing the possibility of further border trouble. In February, in a Peking broadcast, the Ministry of Land Reclamation appealed to the workers in China's border provinces to prepare for battle to protect the nation's frontiers. Workers were asked to "grasp a rifle in one hand and a hoe in the other" to increase production and combat efforts of "reactionaries inside and outside China" to destroy Mao Tse-tung's Cultural Revolution.[24] Anti-Mao sentiment reportedly was particularly strong in the border provinces, in Sinkiang, Inner Mongolia, and Manchuria; armed resistance was said to have broken out. Taking advantage of the confusion in China, and reflecting the Soviet regime's support of the anti-Mao forces, Radio

22 *The New York Times,* September 14, 1964.
23 *The New York Times,* November 22, 1966.
24 *The New York Times,* February 22, 1967.

Moscow sharply stepped up its propaganda broadcasts in Mandarin as well as in the languages of the minorities. The life led by the minorities in Soviet Central Asia was painted in glowing terms. Thus, by mid-1967, the border issue remained a major factor in the Sino-Soviet dispute. The Soviet regime continued to stress its intention of defending its far-flung boundary with China. The Chinese Communists, for their part, seemed in no hurry to relinquish their claims to territories lost in the past to Russia.

IMPLICATIONS OF THE SINO-SOVIET BOUNDARY PROBLEMS FOR EASTERN EUROPE

The Chinese Communist territorial claims against Soviet Russia literally opened a Pandora's box for the USSR. As Radio Moscow observed in a German-language broadcast to Germany on September 3, 1964:

The dangerous evolution of the views and practical policies of the Peking leaders is reflected in Mao Tse-tung's conversation with a group of Japanese socialists.* This conversation is the embodiment in concentrated form of the irrational lust for war, of nationalism and chauvinism.

The leader of the Chinese Communist Party is now advancing claims against the territory of other states. He is trying to fabricate so-called territorial issues between the socialist countries. Such a provocative call for a revision of frontiers can please only the exponents of the most extremist forces of international reaction. Significantly, elements in militarist circles in Bonn and Japan immediately began to stir—elements long bent upon obtaining a revision of treaties and agreements made at the end of the last war after the smashing of Hitler fascism and Japanese militarism.[25]

---

* The conversation—with a five-man group of parliamentary deputies from the Japanese Socialist Party—occurred on July 10, 1964 in Peking.—W.A.D.J.

[25] Quoted in Doolin, *op cit.*, p. 57.

Such a statement may have sought to justify Soviet territorial acquisitions—in Eastern Europe and in the Far East—at the expense of the defeated powers, but in so doing it drew attention to the problem of postwar boundaries generally. In Eastern Europe, in particular, this is a matter of some concern to the Communists, for in the immediate postwar period some fairly drastic revisions were made. "There are border problems which cannot be subject to political talks of a political deal," stated Alexei Adzhubei * and other editors in *Izvestiya*, August 10, 1964.[26] "This refers primarily to the frontiers which took shape in Europe after World War II." Referring to all Soviet frontiers, the writers went on to proclaim: "There can be no appeal to sentimentality in this matter. Here justice triumphs, which is expressed for us in the single word which can be remembered all our lives—victory."

In the postwar readjustment, not only did the Soviet Union push its boundary westward at the expense of many of its satellites, but Germany surrendered its eastern region—beyond the Oder-Neisse Rivers—to Polish administration and East Prussia to Soviet-Polish partition. However real the concern among the East European Communists over the potential threat of a resurgent Germany, it is not the German boundary question alone that must disturb Moscow. China's claims have also provoked the People's Republic of Rumania to challenge the status of the Moldavian SSR, one of the constituent republics of the Soviet Union, and ethnically Rumanian in composition.

Soviet hegemony in Eastern Europe since 1948 has made for boundary stability, although it has not eliminated national feelings and historic rivalries. Even so, Rumania's presentation of a claim to Moldavia, or historic Bessarabia, does come as something of a surprise because of the comparative strength of the two socialist states.

* The son-in-law of Nikita Khrushchev.
[26] *Ibid.*, pp. 46–47.

The Russians gained Bessarabia in 1812, taking it from the Turks. Throughout the rest of the 19th century and until the Bolshevik coup in Russia, Bessarabia remained a Russian province, save for a period between 1856 and 1878 when southern Bessarabia was a part of the principality of Moldavia on its western border. During the upheaval in Russia in 1917–19, the Bessarabians sought independence, but the region was occupied by troops of the Kingdom of Rumania and subsequently annexed. The Treaty of Paris in 1920 recognized Rumanian sovereignty over Bessarabia, an arrangement never accepted by Soviet Russia. In an attempt to woo the Bessarabians, Moscow established along the left-bank Dniester within the Ukrainian Republic a small "autonomous" Moldavian state. This example of Soviet freedom and equality had little appeal for the Bessarabians. But little matter. In the summer of 1940, the Red Army crossed the Dniester, and Bessarabia was annexed to the Soviet Union. The Moldavian ASSR was abolished and a Moldavian SSR was created, extending from the Dniester westward to the Prut. The southern portion, facing the Black Sea, was separated from the rest of Bessarabia and incorporated into the Ukraine as Izmail Oblast.

In 1947 the Soviet Treaty of Peace with Rumania recognized the international boundary established in 1940. Two years later the final demarcation of the line was completed and confirmed in a treaty of February 27, 1961.

The historic population of Bessarabia is predominantly Rumanian in ethnic origin, but with minorities of Jews, Ukrainians, Russians, and other mixed peoples. Under the tsars the native Bessarabians were essentially a peasant people, the landed estates being owned by Russian or Ukrainian gentry. The annexation of the province by Rumania after World War I caused economic dislocation and was not greeted with unbridled enthusiasm by the Bessarabians. On the other hand, the latter showed little interest in communism and were probably further alienated from Soviet Russia during the

1930's as they witnessed the imposition of collectivization across the Dniester in the Moldavian ASSR.[27]

Annexation to the USSR has permitted Bessarabia—as the Moldavian SSR—to join the Soviet family of nations. This has brought both advantages and disadvantages. Collectivization and the transportation of Bessarabians into the Soviet Union have changed both the face of the rural landscape and the complexion of the population.[28] On the other hand, the region has the opportunities which the larger market area of the Union can offer.

It is not clear on what basis the Rumanians may press their right to Bessarabia. Despite the events of the past century or so, the Rumanians seem to be presenting a case that parallels that of the Chinese in their claims to Soviet territory—namely that Imperial Russia seized territory belonging to another. Indeed, late in 1964, there were published in Bucharest some older writings of Marx, unearthed in the Archives of the Second International in Amsterdam, in which he accused Imperial Russia of unlawfully holding

---

[27] For a Soviet account of the history of Bessarabia-Moldavia, see A. L. Odud, *Moldavskaya SSSR,* Moscow, 1955, pp. 4 ff. A good early Western account is given by Charles U. Clark, *Bessarabia,* New York: Dodd, Mead & Co., 1927, pp. 10–91.

[28] There were reports that the Soviet regime had caused Bessarabians or Moldavians to be moved out of the border region in 1944–45, in 1955–56, and again in 1965. According to the Communist Party newspaper in Kishinev, Moldavia, *Moldova Socialista* (January 9, 22, and 29—reported by the London Observer Service in *The Globe and Mail,* Toronto, Canada, February 24, 1965), a general directorate for the recruitment and transfer of workers had been set up. The Soviet objective in this "voluntary" recruitment and transfer of workers was to remove large numbers of Bessarabian farm and factory civil servants to Pavlodar Oblast in Kazakhstan, 3,000 miles to the east. Bucharest reports, on the other hand, were said to indicate that Soviet authorities were putting great pressure on young, well-educated, skilled, and nationally conscious Greater Rumanians, who had resisted Soviet indoctrination.

Bessarabia within the empire. Needless to say, the texts have been widely read in Rumania.[29]

If the Rumanians have a basis for challenging the status of Bessarabia, they are in a shakier position with respect to northern Bukovina, now a part of the Ukraine. This small territory came into the Austro-Hungarian Empire and was never a part of Imperial Russia. With the collapse of the empire of the Danube during World War I, northern Bukovina passed to Rumania. It, like Bessarabia, was occupied by the Soviet Red Army in 1940, and subsequently incorporated into the Ukraine.

In pressing its claims to Bessarabia and nothern Bukovina,[30] Rumania may find itself faced with a renewal of the historic dispute with Hungary over Transylvania. Though in recent years the Rumanian government has made concessions to Hungarian residents in Transylvania in an effort to satisfy their needs, much resentment exists between the Rumanians and the Hungarians.[31] The matter is of obvious concern to the regime in Budapest.

If less than successful in achieving agreement with the Hungarians, the Rumanians seem to enjoy good relations with the Bulgarians and to have taken steps to cooperate with the Yugoslavs. The Rumanian-Bulgarian boundary, drawn at the end of the last war, is essentially an ethnic one and not likely to create difficulties. With the Yugoslavs, there is a plan for joint development of the power resources at the Iron Gate on the Danube.

What the outcome of the Rumanian position will be remains to be seen. Undoubtedly, it has taken much courage to tweak the nose

[29] Ghita Ionescu, "Communist Rumania and Nonalignment, April 1964–March 1965," *Slavic Review*, XXIV, No. 2, June, 1965, p. 252.

[30] The Rumanian Communist leader, Nicolai Ceausescu, in a speech of May 7, 1966, however, refrained from exacerbating the quarrel over Bessarabia, while emphasizing Rumania's right to national independence. Ceausescu did not resign Rumanian claims but left the impression of a "residual claim" to Bessarabia and Bukovina. *The New York Times,* May 28, 1966.

[31] *The New York Times,* February 5, 1966.

of the Russian bear, particularly when the bear is also being pinched by the Chinese in the rear. Rumania would not have been so bold, though, had the moment not been opportune. If allowed to persist in its claims, will Rumania not have set in motion forces which, feeding on the growing nationalism of the region, may lead to increasing tension in Europe and pose a new threat to the Soviet western borderlands?

THE COURSE OF THE
MONGOLIAN PEOPLE'S REPUBLIC

The deterioration of Sino-Soviet state and party relations has had a direct bearing on the position of the Mongol Republic vis-à-vis both the Soviet Union and Communist China. The general line of Mongol foreign policy, stated in mid-1963 in Peking by Professor Dondog Tsevegmid, the ambassador, is peaceful coexistence between countries of different social systems, "as set forth by Lenin." [32] Therefore, in the ideological dispute, the MPR has officially sided with the Soviet Union. Still, it is clear that Ulan Bator is not disposed to assume its former position of total dependence on Moscow. Soviet aid is essential to Mongol economic growth, but the Mongols value participation in COMECON and trade exchanges with other countries.

Within the republic the Mongol leaders have sought to steer a course which upholds independence but does not encourage or permit too vocal an expression of national sentiment. Since nationalism is usually identified with the "cult" of Genghis Khan, every manifestation of it is suppressed. Thus, the party historian, Professor D. Tumur-Ochir, was dismissed from his important post in the fall of 1962 for wanting to call a national festival (which would have been held in May, 1961) to celebrate the eight-hundreth anniversary of Genghis' birth.[33] Not only is it feared

[32] *The London Times*, July 13, 1963.
[33] *The New York Times*, November 2, 1962.

that the cult may undermine the friendly relationship between Outer Mongolia and the Soviet Union, but its suppression is necessary to counteract the influence of Peking, which has tended to encourage the memory of Genghis in Inner Mongolia.

In other areas the split between the CPR and the Soviet Union has left its imprint in Mongolia. There is little evidence, for example, that the treaty signed in December, 1962, formally fixing the 2700-mile long Sino-Mongolian boundary, has ever been implemented. Moreover, the termination of Chinese economic assistance in 1964 made it difficult for the Mongols to fulfill the targets of the Third Five-Year Plan. Under the fourth plan (1966–70), industrial output is to be doubled, but the implementation of the plan depends essentially on Soviet aid provided for under a treaty signed in Ulan Bator, August 4, 1965.[34] By 1970, the Mongols hope also to bring water to some 300 million acres of pasture, but it remains to be seen what can be accomplished even with Soviet help.

The withdrawal of Chinese laborers from the MPR in 1964 was followed by reports in the Western press that Chinese Communist troops were massing along the border. The Mongols accused Peking of trying to turn Mongolia into "an outlying region under Chinese power." [35] The content of the July conversation between Mao and the Japanese socialists was also observed in Ulan Bator. "The desire of the Chinese leaders," reported Montsame, the Mongolian News Agency, "to convert the Mongolian People's Republic into a province of China in effect does in no way differ from the predatory policy of the Chinese landlords and militarists, the Kuomintang reactionaries who are zealous opponents of the sovereignty of the Mongolian people. . . ." Not content with that, Montsame went on to liken the policies of the CPR to those of the imperial dynasty. "The Chinese leaders' claims to Mongolia, whose history of state-

[34] *Mongolia Today,* Aug.–Sept., 1965, p. 1; May, 1966, p. 3.
[35] *The New York Times,* September 10, 1964.

hood has its roots in ancient times, are a result of the great power policy, inherited from the Manchu-Chinese conquerors." [36]

In tone and style Mongolian charges against Peking have resembled those emanating from Alma-Ata in Kazakhstan, as well as directly from Moscow. The Chinese Communists have refrained from engaging in bitter Mongol name-calling, other than to criticize the dependence of Ulan Bator on Moscow. Still the tension remains. Early in 1966 the ties between the USSR and the CPR were officially reaffirmed when L. I. Brezhnev, the First Secretary of the Communist Party of the Soviet Union, led a delegation to Ulan Bator for discussions which resulted in pledges of mutual aid and assistance.[37]

[36] *Mongolia Today,* Sept.–Oct., 1964, pp. 4–5.
[37] *Pravda,* January 18, 1966.

Summary

T HE rapid deterioration of Sino-Soviet state and party relations has revealed to the world at large the existence, beneath the facade of fraternalism, of deep-seated fears and antagonisms which are largely but not entirely the legacy of the past three centuries. The territorial problems which came to light after 1963 best exemplify the extent of the ill feeling found in both the USSR and the CPR. Resentment over historical Russian pressure on Chinese territory has led the Peking regime to claim territories lost by the Manchu emperors, thereby rekindling Soviet concern for its frontiers, in Europe as well as Asia. The boundary question has thus added a new dimension to the Sino-Soviet dispute.

Soviet policy toward China has had much in common with tsarist policy; both sought maximum advantage for Russia from a neighbor whose position remained relatively weaker or ideologically subordinate. Tsarist Russia sought territorial aggrandizement. Not only were vast territories in the Far East and Inner Asia taken from China and incorporated into the Russian Empire, but special privileges were sought and obtained in the remaining border provinces—Manchuria, Outer Mongolia, and Sinkiang. Had the revolution not toppled the Romanovs, it is conceivable that the tsars would have proceeded to annex these territories.

Although Soviet Russia surrendered its special privileges in China generally, it succeeded at the very same time in converting the Chinese province of Outer Mongolia into the Mongolian People's Republic, the first satellite of the new Soviet Union. While the rising power of Japan was instrumental in removing Soviet influence in Manchuria during the 1930's, Moscow played a very prominent role in the affairs of Sinkiang right up until World War II. In the 20th century, therefore, China proper has exercised only limited jurisdiction over its borderlands.

The 1945 agreement between Stalin and Chiang brought still another variation in the traditional pattern of Russo-Chinese relations. While pledging cooperation to Chiang in his efforts to unify Greater China, Stalin nevertheless proceeded to rape Manchurian industry and to seek further privileges in Sinkiang. Even with the revolution that brought the Communists to power in Peking, Moscow still looked forward to a dependent China. Russian influence remained an important element in both Manchuria and Sinkiang until the mid-1950's, and survived in Sinkiang even long after the joint Sino-Soviet enterprises were abolished. Moscow, too, may have sought to use to its advantage the unrest among the Chinese Turkic minorities. Finally, Peking's effort to gain for itself a special place in Outer Mongolia seems to have met so far with disappointment and failure.

During the 1950's, ideological unity tended to obscure the implications of these developments. As the dispute deepened, Chinese reaction to internal Soviet developments and to its search for a detente with the West provoked the Soviet leaders into statements which further irritated Chinese sensitivity, paving the way for a polemic bordering on the absurd. Clearly, the Russians and Chinese were capable of emotions which were not unlike those of old-fashioned nationalism. What was true of the USSR and the CPR was true also of the Communist bloc as a whole. Nationalism was, indeed, a major centrifugal force.

There is little evidence to support the notion that China views its lost territories in the USSR or, for that matter, any part of Asiatic Russia as a whole, as an outlet for its dynamic population. The carrying capacity of the lands immediately bordering China on the north and west are relatively low and offer little promise under present technology.

If not essentially geographical, China's claims to lost territories represent a useful psychological weapon. Peking may not expect to compel a Soviet surrender, but the Chinese leaders may anticipate some boundary rectification. Also, they have served notice on Moscow that Russian pressure on the Chinese borderlands—Sinkiang and Manchuria—must come to an end. For their part, the Russians intend to stand firm behind their "historically-determined" frontiers in Asia and to preserve their special role in the MPR.

Though the China of the "cultural revolution" seems in no position to contemplate or organize military action against the Soviet Union, there remains nevertheless the danger that if the split is irrevocable, at some time in the future war could ensue. On the other hand, the Western World should not be surprised to see Sino-Soviet cooperation on issues concerning which Peking and Moscow are willing to cooperate. Such cooperation undoubtedly affords the Western World less of an opportunity than a challenge or a threat.

Postscript

T HROUGHOUT the latter half of 1967 there were reports in the Western press of Red Army movements in Mongolia and along the Amur. Accounts of Soviet plans to push the economic development of the Trans-Baykal area reflected the growing Soviet concern for its borderlands.

In the October 4, 1967 issue of *Literaturnaya Gazeta* (Literary Gazette), however, the Soviet commentator, Ernst Genri, raised the spectre of Chinese Communist imperialism in terms seldom discussed in the Soviet Union. In referring to "The Great Strategic Plan" of Mao Tse-tung—a plan developed by Mao and his followers in the 1950's but only recently so described by Peking—Genri notes that the basic idea of the plan can be reduced to the creation of some kind of a super state which would encompass not only Eastern but also Central and, ultimately, Western Asia. It would require, however, three stages of implementation.

In the first stage, the Chinese Communists would incorporate Korea, Outer Mongolia, Vietnam, Cambodia, Laos, Indonesia, Malaysia, Burma, and some other countries of the region. This would be followed by the second stage which would result in the incorporation of the Indo-Pakistan peninsula, the Near East, Soviet Central Asia, and the Soviet Far East. What on paper represents the third stage is not, according to Genri, completely clear yet, but it has few limits.

The plan's formula, however, is prophetic: "The today of China is the tomorrow of the whole world."

None of this, notes Genri, will come about without a third world war, but the Maoists anticipate that such a war will lead to victory for China!

During periods of China's weakness, Russia has exercised pressure and secured territorial gains and advantages. When China has recovered, there has been a tendency to hold the line if not to push back. Viewed historically, the present Sino-Soviet difficulties represent, in part, just that. However, in the light of Mao's strategic plan, Chinese pressure assumes a character that bodes ill not only for the Soviet Union but for all Asia and, consequently, for the entire world.

Appendix

RUSSO-CHINESE INTERNATIONAL BOUNDARY
TREATIES AND AGREEMENTS

REATIES instrumental in determining the present boundaries between the USSR, the CPR, and the MPR go back to the Treaty of Nerchinsk in 1689, which was the first treaty ever signed between China and a European country. The most recent alteration in the boundary occurred during World War II, when the Soviet government annexed the Tannu-Tuva People's Republic in 1944, a former province of Outer Mongolia (and thus of China), which had been theoretically independent since the latter part of the 1920's, but in a practical sense had been no more than a Soviet satellite.

Major treaties and agreements since 1689, which pertain to the boundaries, are listed chronologically, by zones:

FAR EAST AND MONGOLIA

August, 1689. Treaty of Nerchinsk. Under the terms of the treaty, it was agreed that the boundary between the Russian and Chinese Empires would extend from the Argun River, continuing along the Amur to the mouth of one of its tributaries, the Kerbechi, thence along the Kerbechi to the outer Khingan Mountains, i.e., along the Yablonovoy and Stanovoy Mountains, to the source of the Ud River, which flows into the Sea of Okhotsk. All of the southern slopes of the Stanovoy Mountains with rivers flowing into the

Amur were to belong to China, while all northern slopes with rivers flowing to the north were ceded to Russia. The boundary through the Ud Valley was not decided, and it remained neutral territory. All Russian ostrogs (posts) on the Amur, including the Russian post at Albazin, were to be destroyed, and no Russian colonists were permitted to settle on Manchurian territory beyond the river. Those already established there had to leave or become Chinese citizens. In all, the Chinese ceded about 93,000 square miles to the Russians.

April, 1727. Russo-Chinese Agreement in Peking. The agreement specified that the frontier from the Bay of Ud to the Stanovoy Mountains would remain undecided as in the Treaty of Nerchinsk, owing to the lack of definite topographical information concerning the region; but elsewhere the boundary would be determined by a joint Russo-Chinese border commission.

October, 1727. Treaty of Kiakhta. Under the terms of the treaty, the boundary was fixed between Mongolia and Siberia, from the Sayan Mountains and Sapintabakha (Shaban-Dabeg), a pass through the Sayan, in the west to the Argun River in the east (Article 3). The commission, however, was unclear in defining the border in the vicinity of Urianghay, or Tuva. As far as the Russians were concerned, as they later were to claim, the allegiance of Tuva remained undetermined. Nevertheless, according to Count Sava Vladislavich Roguzinskiy, the Russian envoy at Kiakhta, ". . . the newly established frontier is highly advantageous to Russia and . . . actually the Russian possessions have been extended into Mongolia a distance of several days' march, and, in certain sections, of even several weeks." For their part, the Chinese lost nearly 40,000 square miles, between the Upper Irtysh and the Sayan Mountains, as well as south and southwest of Lake Baykal. The boundary west of the Bay of Ud remained undefined (Article 7).

October, 1768. Kiakhta Supplementary Treaty. Article 10 of the Treaty of Kiakhta was amended to regulate frontier traffic. Minor changes were also made in the vicinity of boundary posts.

May, 1858. Treaty of Aigun. Under the terms of the treaty, China ceded to Russia the left bank of the Amur down to the Ussuri, while the territory on the right bank as far as the Ussuri remained Chinese. The territory between the Ussuri and the Pacific Ocean was to belong in common to Russia and China until decided at a future date. In all, the Chinese surrendered to the Russians about 185,000 square miles of territory.

China was allowed to retain jurisdiction over the Manchu inhabitants on the left bank of the Amur from the Zeya River to the village of Khormoldsin, living in the "Sixty-Four Settlements to the East of the Amur," known as Chiang-Tung-Lu-Shih-Szu-T'un.

June, 1858. Treaty of Tientsin. While the treaty was mainly commercial, it did include an article pertaining to the frontier. It stipulated that frontiers between the two powers not yet decided were to be surveyed. Actually, there was no need for the clause since the Treaty of Aigun embraced this point. However, it was included by the Russian negotiator because he was unaware at the time that the Aigun Treaty had been approved.

November, 1860. Treaty of Peking. According to the treaty, the territory east of the Ussuri to the Pacific (133,000 square miles) was ceded to Russia (Article 1). The boundary between Russia and China was to follow the Ussuri south to and along its tributary, the Songatcha, thence across Lake Khanka to the Korean frontier. Delegates were to be appointed by the Chinese and Russian governments to survey and map the frontier from Lake Khanka to the Tumien River.

October, 1864. Boundary Treaty of Tarbagatay. The treaty was concerned with the boundary between Sinkiang and Russian Turkestan, but it also referred to the Russian-Outer Mongolian boundary through the Sayan Mountains. This document was followed by an additional treaty in 1870, the Treaty of Uliassutay, which similarly referred to the demarcation of the Russian-Outer Mongolian boundary. Later, in 1911, when the question of Mongolia and Urianghay came up in cabinet discussions in St. Petersburg, Sazonov, the tsarist foreign minister, reported that the Treaty of Tarbagatay (or Chuguchak) had clearly defined Urianghay as a part of Chinese territory.

December, 1911. Tsitishar Treaty. This boundary treaty between Russia and China redelimited the boundary from Tarbaga Dagh to Abahaitu, and along the Argun River to its confluence with the Amur River. Under the terms of the treaty, commissions were appointed to fix precisely the international boundary.

The boundary in this sector was originally based on the Treaty of Kiakhta. By the 1911 agreement, however, the Russians extended the boundary into China by about five miles along a 60-mile front, drawn for the most part along the southerly channel of the Argun. Beyond that, differing channels of the Argun were utilized for an additional 40 to 50 miles.

Neither the Republican Government of China nor the Communist regime has recognized the validity of the agreement.

November, 1913. Note to the Chinese Minister for Foreign Affairs, on the Question of Outer Mongolian Autonomy. The Russian minister at Peking argued that Autonomous Outer Mongolia should comprise the regions which have been under the jurisdiction of the Chinese Amban of Urga, of the Tartar-General of Uliassutay, and of the Chinese Amban of Kobdo. Inasmuch as there were no detailed maps of Mongolia and the boundaries of the administrative divisions of the country were uncertain, he agreed that the exact boundaries of Outer Mongolia, as well as the boundary between Mongolia and the district of Altay, should be the subject of the subsequent conferences provided for in Article 5 of the Russo-Chinese Declaration of November 5, 1913.

June, 1915. Russo-Chinese-Mongolian Tripartite Agreement. Under Article 10 of the Agreement, the territory of Autonomous Outer Mongolia was said to comprise the regions which were under the jurisdiction of the Chinese Amban at Urga, of the Tartar-General at Uliassutay, and of the Chinese Amban at Kobdo. It connected with the boundary of China at the limits of the four aimaks of Khalka and of the district of Kobdo, and was bounded by the district of Houlunbouir (i.e., Hailar) on the east, by Inner Mongolia on the south, by the Province of Sinkiang on the southwest, and by the district of Altay on the west.

The formal delimitation between China and Autonomous Outer Mongolia was to be carried out by a special commission of delegates of China, Russia, and Autonomous Outer Mongolia, which would commence its work within a period of two years.

In the struggle over Outer Mongolian "independence" in 1911, the Mongols in the Altay district had not supported the rest of the province. Because of their loyalty to China, the Republican Government of China detached the region from Outer Mongolia and incorporated it in Sinkiang in 1919.

November, 1921. Agreement for Establishing Friendly Relations Between Soviet Russia and Outer Mongolia. Under the terms of the agreement, the frontier between Russia and Outer Mongolia was to be established by a special commission, agreed to by the Russian Republic and Mongolia. However, Urianghay, the northwestern province of Mongolia, although claimed as part of its territory by Mongolia, was not acknowledged as such by the Russians.

May, 1924. Agreement on General Principles for the Settlement of the Questions between the Republic of China and the USSR. Article 7 of the agreement pledged the two countries to redemarcate their national boundaries at a conference to be held within one month after the signing of the agreement and, pending such redemarcation, to maintain their common boundary.

August, 1926. Treaty of Friendship between the People's Republic of Tannu-Tuva and the Mongolian People's Republic. In the agreement, the governments, under Soviet pressure, recognized their separation and each other's independence. Because of Outer Mongolia's opposition to the loss of Urianghay, the Soviets arranged to have Darkhat, a small, sparsely inhabited strip of territory west of Lake Khobso Gol, transferred from Urianghay to Mongolia.

December, 1962. Sino-Mongolian Boundary Agreement. Under the agreement, the boundary between the MPR and the CPR was to be formally fixed.

CENTRAL ASIA

November, 1860. Treaty of Peking. The treaty, in those sections pertaining to Turkestan, specified that the boundary between Russia and China should be based upon the then-existing line of permanent pasture pickets, which the Chinese had established to limit the use of pastures by the nomadic Kazakhs. Commissioners were to be appointed by the Chinese and Russian governments to survey and map the frontier from Shaban-Dabeg to the Kokan's possessions (Kokand). In effect, China surrendered her claim to nearly 350,000 square miles.

October, 1864. Treaty of Tarbagatay. Under the terms of the treaty, which was hastily concluded because of an Islamic revolt in Sinkiang, the boundary was drawn along the line of permanent pickets, as agreed on at Peking in 1860.

(In attempting to regulate the use of pastures, China had established two types of pickets—permanent and movable. The Chinese commissioners contended that the boundary line should be drawn along the outermost, movable pickets; whereas the Russians insisted that it should follow the line of permanent pickets as provided in the Treaty of Peking. Thus, at Tarbagatay, the Chinese ceded extensive tracts of land, over which, however, they had held little more than a regulatory control.)

The boundary was, therefore, fixed as following the mountains, great rivers, and the existing line of Chinese permanent pickets. It ran from the lighthouse at Shaban-Dabeg southwestward to Lake Zaysan, thence to the mountains situated to the south of Lake Issyk-Kul and "along these mountains as far as the Kokan's possessions" (Article 2).

(Later, between 1869 and 1870, the boundary lines in the Kobdo, Uliassutay, and Tarbagatay regions of Mongolia and Sinkiang, as noted above, were defined and boundary stakes set up. When, in 1870, the boundary was staked at Tarbagatay, the Russians planted some stakes in Chinese territory, intruding for another score of miles and cutting the main thoroughfare between Tarbagatay and Altay.)

February, 1881. Treaty of St. Petersburg. In July, 1870, the Russians occupied the upper Ili River Valley on the pretext of maintaining law and order during the local Islamic revolt against Chinese administration. The Chinese were unable to put down the revolt or to compel the Russians to leave the Ili.

(In July, 1879, in the Treaty of Livadia, signed by the Chinese delegate in St. Petersburg but never ratified by the Chinese government, the Chinese agreed under the terms of the treaty to cede the Tekes Valley and the strategic passes through the Tien-Shan, including the route to Kashgar. In return, Russia promised to withdraw from the rest of the Ili region.)

Under the terms of the Treaty of St. Petersburg, which was ratified by Peking, the Russians agreed to return to China the Ili Valley occupied in 1871, with China retaining also the Tekes Valley and the passes through the Tien-Shan. A small area west of the Holkuts River was ceded to Russia (Article 7) for the purpose of settling the emigrants from Chinese Turkestan—that is, those inhabitants of Chinese territory who preferred to live under Russian rule.

According to Article 6, the Chinese emperor was required to pay, within two years, nine million rubles in silver, to compensate for the military expenses incurred by Russia in suppressing the disorder in the Ili and the losses suffered there by Russian merchants and families.

According to Article 8, the boundary lines east of Lake Zaysan and west of Kashgar, as determined by the Treaty of Tarbagatay, were to be redemarcated. (In the boundary agreements that followed —in August, 1862, concerning the southern boundary of the Ili; in November, 1882, concerning Kashgar; in July, 1883, concerning Kobdo and Tarbagatay; and in May, 1885, concerning Kashgar— China lost more than 15,000 square miles of territory to Russia.)

Russia had been allowed by the Treaty of Livadia to establish consulates in the Ili Valley, especially at Ili, and at Tarbagatay. By the Treaty of St. Petersburg, additional consulates were permitted.

March, 1895. Agreement between Great Britain and Russia, with Regard to the Spheres of Influence of the Two Countries in the Region of the Pamirs. (The Russian advance into Central Asia alarmed the British, who were concerned for the security of India. In 1873, however, the Russians agreed to accept the course of the Amu-Darya [Oxus] between its source in Lake Zar-Kul in the Pamirs to a point where the river turns northward [near long. 66°E] as the northern boundary of Afghanistan. When the British withdrew from Afghanistan after the Second Afghan War, for all practical purposes Afghanistan became a buffer state between the two major powers.

(In the meantime, after the Chinese had recovered control of Sinkiang, they established in 1878 their frontier posts in the Pamirs. But the rugged nature of the terrain prevented any precise demarcation.

(In 1891, the tsar dispatched troops to the eastern Pamirs to protect Russian scientific expeditions. Alarmed by this new advance, Britain then invaded Hunza, a mountainous state southeast of Wakhan owing allegiance to China. The Chinese government protested, to no avail. In order to secure the northwest frontier of India against Russia, Britain made an effort to secure Chinese participation in a boundary agreement. Since no agreement was forthcoming, Britain and Russia came to terms on a Pamir boundary. Afghanistan, under British pressure, agreed to accept the narrow Wakhan Valley, which would thus prevent contiguity between Russia and British India.)

In the summer of 1895, according to the terms of the Anglo-Russian agreement of the preceding March, demarcation of the Russian-Afghanistan boundary took place. The line was drawn eastward from Lake Zar-Kul along the crest of mountains to the valley of the Ak-Su, thence eastward through the valley for two miles. From that point, it turned southeast for six miles, where it reached a rugged and inaccessible spur of the Sarikol Range.

Bibliography

A Regional Handbook on Northwest China, New Haven, HRAF Press, 1956, 2 vols.

Max Beloff, *Soviet Policy in the Far East, 1944–51,* London, Oxford University Press, 1953.

Edward M. Bennett (ed.), *Polycentrism: Growing Dissidence in the Communist Bloc?* Pullman, Washington State University Press, 1967.

Howard L. Boorman and others, *Moscow-Peking Axis: Strengths and Strains,* New York, Harper & Bros., 1957.

Olaf Caroe, *Soviet Empire: The Turks of Central Asia and Stalinism,* London, Macmillan & Co.,1953.

Edward Hallett Carr, *The Bolshevik Revolution, 1917–1923,* Vol. 1, New York, Macmillan & Co., 1951.

Cheng Tien-fong, *A History of Sino-Soviet Relations,* Washington, Public Affairs Press, 1957.

O. Edmund Clubb, *Chinese Communist Development Programs in Manchuria,* New York, Institute of Pacific Relations, 1954.

George B. Cressey, *Land of the 500 Million: A Geography of China,* New York, McGraw-Hill Book Co., Ltd., 1955.

David J. Dallin, *Soviet Russia and the Far East,* New Haven, Yale University Press, 1948.

David J. Dallin, *The Rise of Russia in Asia,* New Haven, Yale University Press, 1949.

Dennis J. Doolin, *Territorial Claims in the Sino-Soviet Conflict. Documents and Analyses,* Hoover Institution Studies: 7, Stanford, 1965.

W. Gordon East and A. E. Moodie (eds.), *The Changing World: Studies in Political Geography,* London, George G. Harrap & Co., Ltd., 1956.

Herbert Feis, *The China Tangle,* New York, Atheneum, 1965.

Louis Fischer, *The Soviets in World Affairs,* Princeton, Princeton University Press, 1951, 2 vols.

David Floyd, *Mao Against Khrushchev. A Short History of the Sino-Soviet Conflict,* New York, Praeger, 1963.

Gerard M. Friters, *Outer Mongolia and Its International Position,* Baltimore, Johns Hopkins University Press, 1949.

Elliot R. Goodman, *The Soviet Design for a World State,* New York, Columbia University Press, 1960.

William E. Griffith, *The Sino-Soviet Rift,* Cambridge, The M.I.T. Press, 1964.

Ho Ping-ti, *Studies on the Population of China, 1368–1953,* Cambridge, Mass., Harvard University Press, 1959.

Charles W. Hostler, *Turkism and the Soviets,* New York, Frederick A. Praeger, 1957.

Hsiao Hsia (ed.), *China: Its People, Its Society, Its Culture,* New Haven, HRAF Press, 1960.

G. F. Hudson and Marthe Rajchman, *An Atlas of Far Eastern Politics,* London, Faber and Faber Ltd., 1938.

International Boundary Study. No. 64—Feb. 14, 1966, *China-USSR Boundary.* Issued by the Geographer. Office of Research in Economics and Science, Bureau of Intelligence and Research, Department of State, Washington, D.C.

George F. Kennan, *Russia and the West under Lenin and Stalin,* Boston, Little, Brown & Co., 1961.

E. Stuart Kirby (ed.), *Contemporary China, 1961–1962,* Hong Kong, University Press, 1963.

Walter Kolarz, *Russia and Her Colonies,* London, George Phillips & Son Ltd., 1952.

Walter Kolarz, *The Peoples of the Soviet Far East,* New York, Frederick A. Praeger, 1954.

Owen Lattimore, *The Mongols of Manchuria,* New York, The John Day Co., 1934.

Owen Lattimore, *Manchuria: Cradle of Conflict,* 2nd ed., New York, Macmillan & Co., 1935.

Owen Lattimore, *Inner Asian Frontiers of China,* New York, American Geographical Society, 1940, 1951.

Owen Lattimore, *Nationalism and Revolution in Mongolia,* New York, Oxford University Press, 1955.

Prince A. Lobanov-Rostovsky, *Russia and Asia,* Ann Arbor, G. Wahr Publ. Co., 1951. (Originally published by Macmillan, N.Y., 1933.)

Sir Halford J. Mackinder, *Democratic Ideals and Reality. A Study in the Politics of Reconstruction,* New York, Henry Holt & Co., 1919, 1942.

Manchuria. Treaties and Agreements, Washington, Carnegie Endowment for International Peace, 1921.

William M. McGovern, *The Early Empires of Central Asia,* Chapel Hill, University of North Carolina Press, 1939.

Klaus Mehnert, *Peking and Moscow,* New York, G. P. Putnam's Sons, 1963.

Alexandre Metaxas, *Pekin Contre Moscow,* Lausanne, Editions Scriptar, 1959.

Franz H. Michael and George E. Taylor, *The Far East in the Modern World,* New York, Henry Holt & Co., 1956.

Mongolian People's Republic, New Haven, HRAF Press, 1956, 3 vols.

George Moseley, *A Sino-Soviet Cultural Frontier,* East Asian Research Center, Harvard University, 1966.

George G. S. Murphy, *Soviet Mongolia: A Study of the Oldest Political Satellite,* Berkeley and Los Angeles, University of California Press, 1966.

Outer Mongolia. Treaties and Agreements, Washington, Carnegie Endowment for International Peace, 1921.

Alexander G. Park, *Bolshevism in Turkestan, 1917–1927,* New York, Columbia University Press, 1957.

Richard A. Pierce, *Russian Central Asia, 1867–1917,* Berkeley and Los Angeles, University of California Press, 1960.

Richard Pipes, *The Formation of the Soviet Union: Communism and Nationalism, 1917–1923,* Cambridge, Mass., Harvard University Press, 1954.

John Rowland, *A History of Sino-Indian Relations. Hostile Co-Existence,* Princeton, D. Van Nostrand Co., Inc., 1967.

Harrison E. Salisbury, *To Moscow—and Beyond,* New York, Harper & Bros., 1959.

Theodore Shabad, *Geography of the USSR, A Regional Survey*, New York, Columbia University Press, 1951.

Theodore Shabad, *China's Changing Map*, New York, Frederick A. Praeger, 1956.

Edgar Snow, *Red Star Over China*, New York, Random House, 1938.

Peter S. H. Tang, *Communist China Today*, New York, Frederick A. Praeger, 1957, 1958, 2 vols.

Peter S. H. Tang, *Russian and Soviet Policy in Manchuria and Outer Mongolia, 1911–1931*, Durham, Duke University Press, 1959.

John E. Tashjean, *Where China Meets Russia: An Analysis of Dr. Starlinger's Theory*, Central Asian Collectanea, No. 2, Washington, 1959.

The Travels of Marco Polo, New York, Boni and Liveright, 1926.

Erich Thiel, *The Soviet Far East, A Survey of Its Physical and Economic Geography*, New York, Frederick A. Praeger, 1957.

Treaties and Agreements with and Concerning China, 1894–1919, Washington, Carnegie Endowment for International Peace, 1921, 2 vols.

Treaties and Agreements with and Concerning China, 1919–1929, Washington, Carnegie Endowment for Internatioal Peace, 1929.

Allen S. Whiting, *Soviet Policies in China, 1917–1924*, New York, Columbia University Press, 1954.

Allen S. Whiting and General Sheng Shih-ts'ai, *Sinkiang: Pawn or Pivot?* East Lansing, Michigan State University Press, 1958.

Aitchen K. Wu, *China and the Soviet Union. A Study of Sino-Soviet Relations*, New York, The John Day Co., 1950.

Victor A. Yakhontoff, *Russia and the Soviet Union in the Far East*, London, Allen & Unwin, 1932.

C. Walter Young, *The International Relations of Manchuria*, Chicago, University of Chicago Press, 1929.

Index

Afghanistan, 9, 144, 145
agriculture
  in China, 89
  in Manchuria, 26, 88–89
  in Mongolia, 95–97
  in Siberia, 107–108
  in Sinkiang, 20
  in Soviet Far East, 28, 108
Aigun, Treaty of, 24, 46, 117, 139
air transport, 81, 91
Aktogay, 15, 16, 91
Alma-Ata, 14, 16, 22, 48, 62, 81
Altay Mountains, 7–8, 16, 30, 32, 33, 34
Amur Basin, 39, 41, 90, 104
Amur Oblast, 25
Amur River, 8, 23, 24, 26, 27, 40, 41, 52, 90, 103, 122
Ancient China, 38
Aral Sea, 8, 91
Argun River, 23, 24, 34, 43, 46
Astrakhan, 40

Balkhash, Lake, 14, 48, 55
Baykal, Lake, 7, 34, 43, 46, 51, 55, 57, 58, 138
Baykal-Amur Railway, 59
Baykalia, 42
Berg, L. S., 10
Bessarabia, 125–128
Birobidzhan, 26
Bolshevik Revolution, 12, 55, 56, 59, 102, 118, 120
borderlands
  Chinese Communist reorganization of, 82–87

borderlands (*cont.*)
  dispute, implications for Eastern Europe, 124–129
  Far Eastern Sector, 23–29
  geographical characteristics, 7–37
  history of, 38–66
  Inner Asian Sector, 7–23
  Mongolian Sector, 7, 29–38
boundary, Russo-Chinese (*see* borderlands)
Boxer Rebellion, 52
Bratsk, 36
Brezhnev, L. I., 131
Bukhara, Emirate of, 11
Bulganin, Nikolai, 81
Buryat-Mongol Autonomous Soviet Socialist Republic, 58
Buryat Mongols, 40, 41, 59

Cambodia, 135
Camp David talks, 113
Catherine the Great, 41
Changchun Railway, 68, 69, 81
Chiang Kai Shek, 65, 68, 69, 70, 72, 74, 75, 87, 133
Chinese Communists, 70, 72, 76, 100, 113, 135
Chinese Eastern Railway, 33, 57, 58, 69, 102, 119
Chinese Empire, 38–39, 101
Chinese languages, 86–87
Chinese-Mongolian Commercial Treaty, 98
Chinese Nationalists, 39, 58, 66, 72, 75, 99, 102, 103, 105